Christians

and a Land Called Holy

How We Can Foster Justice, Peace, and Hope

Charles P. Lutz & Robert O. Smith

To Grace and Will

In solidarity!

Fortress Press
Minneapolis

CHRISTIANS AND A LAND CALLED HOLY
How We Can Foster Justice, Peace, and Hope

Cover photo: © Ricki Rosen/Corbis

About the cover: Of all Holy Land people living between the river and the sea, Muslims and Jews comprise 98 percent and have virtually identical numbers (Christians are a minuscule minority). Is there any promise that young Jews and young Muslims can have a future together marked by mutual respect and affection (with young Christians opting to stay and enter that future of peace and hope)?

Cover and interior design: Becky Lowe

Appendix written by Ron D. Witherup and originally published as an article "Whose Land Is It?" © 2003 Ronald D. Witherup. Used by permission.

Library of Congress Cataloging-in-Publication Data

Lutz, Charles P.
   Christians and a land called holy : how we can foster justice, peace, and hope / Charles P. Lutz, Robert O. Smith.
      p. cm.
   ISBN 0-8006-3784-4 (alk. paper)
   1. Palestine in Christianity. 2. Arab-Israeli conflict—Religious aspects—Christianity. 3. Religion and politics—Palestine. 4. Sacred space—Political aspects—Palestine. 5. Religious fundamentalism—Palestine. 6. Christian Zionism. 7. Christians—Political activity. I. Smith, Robert Ora, 1920- II. Title.

BT93.8.L88 2006
263'.0425694—dc22

                              2005026223

10   09   08   07   06   1   2   3   4   5   6   7   8   9   10

Contents

Quotation from Psalms 122 in Hebrew, Arabic, and English on a building in Old City, Jerusalem.

Pray for the peace of Jerusalem:
"May they prosper who love you.
Peace be within your walls,
and security within your towers."
For the sake of my relatives and friends
I will say, "Peace be within you."
For the sake of the house of the Lord our God,
I will seek your good.

Psalm 122:6-9

There are thousands of years of fighting and hatred, but what I'm hoping is . . . that it can be our generation that puts that aside so that we can all come to the Holy Land in peace.

U.S. First Lady Laura Bush,
after visiting Jerusalem, May 2005

Author Charles Lutz reflecting on rock-reverence of faith communities in Jerusalem's Old City: Jews praying at the Western Wall (of the second temple) and Muslims just above at the Dome of the Rock. A few blocks to the west, Christians honor Golgotha rock inside the Church of the Holy Sepulcher where tradition says Jesus was crucified.

Preface

Christians and a Land Called Holy: How We Can Foster Justice, Peace, and Hope was born as an idea when the authors together visited Israel/Palestine in 2002. That visit reinforced for them two realities: that Christians from elsewhere in the world have a faith-based interest in seeking a just peace between Israelis and Palestinians, and that they have a key role to play in pursuit of that peace.

Together, we reasoned that the world's Christians have a special calling to seek peace for both Israelis and Palestinians. Among the reasons:

- Christians around the world have been making Holy Land pilgrimages for many centuries and long to continue doing so with some assurance of safe passage.
- The indigenous Christians of Palestine and Israel are begging us to become active in their struggle for a secure and just peace.
- We are major supporters of distinctive ministries in that land, ministries that are difficult to sustain in the midst of warring.
- Christians living in the United States are particularly called to citizen advocacy with our own government, which has unsurpassed political and economic influence over the conflicting parties.

With these and many other reasons in mind, it seemed to us that many Christians could benefit from a book that summarizes the present relationship of global Christianity to the peoples of the Holy Land and provides practical tips for acting as peace seekers today.

As with any project of this sort, the authors are indebted to a large number of individuals who have supported and encouraged our work throughout this book's birthing process. They include Pastor Said Ailabouni, a Palestinian-American who is director for Europe and the Middle East with the Division for Global Mission, Evangelical Lutheran Church in America; Corinne Whitlatch, executive director of Churches for Middle East Peace; and Janet Tollund, a sales representative at Group Travel Directors in Minneapolis, Minnesota. Special thanks are due also to Pastor Mary Albing, Michele Bennett, Ann Hafften, Elliot Ratzman, Rabbi Paula Reimers, and Santiago Slabodsky for their editorial suggestions. Portions of chapters 2 and 3 have appeared in articles published by the *Journal of Church and State* and *Koinonia Journal* (Princeton Theological Seminary).

This book presents one portion of the ongoing journeys of the authors toward responsible expression of their Christian discipleship. You hold in your hands the fruit of their partnership at this stage of the journey and an invitation to join them in working for justice with peace in God's world.

Introduction

Lord, make us instruments of your peace.
—*from a prayer attributed to Saint Francis of Assisi*

It's a curious term, *Holy Land*. Does it seek to suggest that one piece of Planet Earth is sacred in a way that other parts are not? That the terra firma found west of the Jordan River and east of the Mediterranean—or "from Dan even to Beersheba" (1 Kings 4:25)—is more favored, more blessed by God than other parts of God's creation?

This language is curious in another way, too. The particular land that has come to be known as "holy," a slim slice about the size of the U.S. state of New Jersey, has surely seen over many millennia as much horrific human conflict as any area of comparable acreage on earth. And yes, nearly all its violence and killing have been carried out by humans explicitly *in the name of God!* And it still goes on.

Why Not "Unholy Land"?

Does that make it a land we should name Holy? A label quite the contrary would seem more fitting. Maybe "unholy land" would make better sense. Or "land where Satan prevails." Or perhaps "godless land"?

Trouble is, the peoples of that land whose stories we've inherited from the past four thousand years have seen themselves

1

precisely as *godly* people. Nearly all of them have, in fact, claimed to be devoted followers of the Holy One, the one true God, the God of Abraham and his heirs. Indeed, that land is exactly where the very idea of monotheism—that God is One—has flowered most fully. Some of these believers would argue that the land is best known not as Holy Land but as Land of the Holy One.

While "holy" and "religious" are not the same, they often get used as synonyms. There surely has been no other place on earth where the passions of faith and politics interplay so totally, with such devotion, and for such a long time. Some would even say, "It's not a matter of politics and faith interacting, as two distinct elements coming together. In the Holy Land, faith and politics are one and the same!"

There is clearly something within communities of Jews, Christians, and Muslims alike that wants to consider this land set apart, blessed or sanctioned or occupied by the Holy One—in a way that other parts of the earth are not. Where does that come from, and what does it mean for believers today?

Christians and This Special Space

And how do Christians especially, Christians who live anywhere in the world, see this particular land as special space? That question and its connection with the seemingly endless dispute between Israelis and Palestinians get preliminary attention in Charles Lutz's chapter 1.

Robert Smith will next explore the overlapping of faith with politics, and the role of religious convictions that are increasingly fundamentalist and thus, by definition, unable to abide any political compromises.

In chapter 3, Smith digs into the deepening division within today's Christian community, between those identifying as Christian Zionists and the rest of us. Are Christians irreparably divided? Can we find, on the question of this land, no common ground?

In the last chapter, Lutz presents the call for Christians to act on matters pertaining to the Holy Land. First is a focus on listening and learning—what we must know and how we may stay constructively informed in a learning arena that is filled with spin and is both theologized and politicized with high emotional intensity. The rest of our call includes a range of specific actions, from praying to public-policy advocating to making pilgrimages and supporting Christian ministries at work in that land.

An appendix—"Whose Land Is It?"—presents Roman Catholic scholar Ronald Witherup's thoughts on the biblical politics of the Holy Land. A resource section offers an annotated list of books, videos, and Web sites designed to help readers engage more thoroughly the issues discussed in this book.

At the Heart Is the Holy City

We trust our readers will find the book helpful, in both the religious and political quests for a just peace between the peoples living on this land today. To what is God calling us on behalf of a land that continues to be so deeply troubled, even as we keep identifying it as a place that is holy? Where can we find hope that the Holy Land can become a land flowing not just with milk and honey but also with justice and peace?

Our scriptures often express this yearning for peace and justice by speaking of Jerusalem, the golden city, the Holy City. Can peace ever come to Jerusalem, the city that writer James Carroll characterizes as the "epicenter of God-sponsored violence"?

But Jerusalem hasn't always been a city of violence and interfaith strife. For more than thirteen centuries (638–1948 CE) Jerusalem enjoyed peace, prosperity, and even religious tolerance that was probably unsurpassed anywhere in the world during those thirteen hundred years. It was a time when Muslims—surprise!—were in control. This long period was interrupted twice, both times by Western (and Christian) power: the hundred years of aggression, killing, and intolerance that marked the Crusades (the twelfth century) and some thirty years of British occupation following World War I (1917–48).

Today, it seems clear to almost everyone that the city at the Holy Land's heart will also be at the heart of any lasting resolution of the conflict. Somehow, a political design that has Jerusalem shared by Israelis and Palestinians (with respective capitals in parts of that city) will be required. And it must be a design that gives all three Abrahamic faith traditions unimpeded access to their respective holy sites in the Holy City.

All reports from the Camp David negotiations under President Bill Clinton in 2000 indicate that finding agreement on the just sharing of Jerusalem was a major stumbling block between Israelis and Palestinians. And so it is today. In the years since 2000, Israeli "facts on the ground"—settlement expansion east of the city, uprooting of Palestinians from historic homes in East Jerusalem, construction of a separation barrier between Jerusalem and the West Bank—have made dismal the prospect of a Jerusalem that is shared by two peoples and three faiths. As Danny Rubinstein wrote in the Israeli newspaper *Ha'aretz* (June 11, 2005):

> Among the Palestinian public—just as among the Israeli public— public opinion surveys show that the majority still favors . . . establishing two countries for the two nations. Eliminating the option of a Palestinian capital in Jerusalem means the end of the two-state solution. . . . What is being done now in Jerusalem is destroying it. And if there are not two nations for two states here, the only other option is one state for two nations. There is nothing else.

In the end, all believers must, with the writer of Isaiah, continue to pray and to hope that the day comes soon when we can "rejoice with Jerusalem . . . all you who mourn over her" (Isaiah 66:10). So we do long for an end to the mourning, among those who dwell there and among all of us who long to rejoice with her.

This hope is not only for Jerusalem. We seek a just peace that radiates out from the Holy City to Judea and Samaria and Galilee, and to the entire community of humankind. There are many signs that for the world to have lasting peace today, this peace must begin in Jerusalem and flow to the ends of the earth.

Going with Francis

It was in 1219, during the Fifth Crusade, that Francis, the layman-monk from Assisi in Italy, went to the Holy Land. Francis was unarmed, accompanying armed fellow Christians from Europe who were fighting to take military control from Muslims. Francis wanted to convert the leader of the Muslim forces to Christianity, thinking this effort would end the warring over control of the holy places. Although he did not succeed in this goal of conversion, Francis's preaching of peace did impress Sultan al-Kamil, and the Muslim leader granted Francis permission to visit the sacred sites in Palestine.

To this day, members of the Franciscan Order are the caretakers of places in the Holy Land associated with the life of Christ. Conservation and restoration of those sites has been the basic reason for Franciscan presence in the region since 1342, when Pope Clement IV institutionalized the mission of Franciscan Custody in the Holy Land. There are twenty-six such sites, and surrounding most of them, the Franciscans have built churches and schools, artisan workshops and housing. All of this has been done while providing social services that benefit Muslims and Christians alike.

Francis wished to "conquer" the holy sites, not through force of arms but through dialogue with governing authorities. Part of his rule reads, "Brothers who go to the Holy Land must not engage in litigation or disputes, must be at the service of all, and manifest with their life that they are Christians."

Francis did not end the fighting in the Holy Land eight centuries ago. But this courageous peace seeker, one of the few Christians of his day who opposed the Crusades' violent tactics, urged Christians to learn from and live harmoniously with people of other faiths. Particularly in their love for this land called holy, Francis wanted all Christians to ask God, in the words of the prayer attributed to him:

Lord, make us instruments of your peace.

This book is dedicated to the pursuit of that peace/*salaam*/*shalom*.

Archway in Jerusalem embodying the distinctive architecture and alluring character of this ancient city. One way to translate the name Jerusalem *is* "City of Peace." *But through the centuries, it has rarely known the peace for which it is named.*

Chapter 1

What's So Special about This Space?

Charles P. Lutz

Christianity has provided a kind of leavening in the Middle East . . . acting as a buffer between the Arab world's broad Islamic resurgence and the strands within Israel of a rising ultranationalist brand of Judaism. These two fundamentalist movements, which have fused religion with nationalism, increasingly cast the territorial Israeli-Palestinian conflict in religious terms. If the Christians disappear, the Middle East will become that much more vulnerable to this embittered dichotomy.

Charles M. Sennott, *The Body and the Blood*

A small piece of territory at the southeast corner of the Mediterranean Sea occupies a special spot in the hearts of many human beings. This affection has existed for thousands of years. It's a land that has distinctive meaning for believers from each of three monotheistic faith traditions. That specific geography, say the heirs of Abraham, has unique content, not just for their historic memory, but within the divine-human relationship itself to this very day.

When they apply the word *holy* to this land, the meaning is not exactly the same for Jews, Muslims, and Christians. Indeed, the understanding of what makes this geography special varies even within each of the three faiths. But believers in all three traditions find it useful—and generally positive—to speak of "holy land" in some sense or another.

For Jews and Muslims

Today's Jews believe this land was promised by God to their ancestors, the ancient Israelites. Modern Jews will disagree on whether to insist it is *by divine right* that the land of today's Israel belongs to Jews. Today's Jews—both in Israel and worldwide—also debate the exact extent of Middle East territory that the state of Israel has a political right to occupy and govern.

But virtually all Jews everywhere concur that a contemporary nation-state known as Israel has a right to exist—where it is—as a homeland for Jews. And they agree that this homeland, in this exact place, has a specific historic connection to the intention of God.

The *holy land* term itself appears only once in the Hebrew Bible (Zechariah 2:12), and there it points to a future, messianic age. More commonly, the biblical way of indicating this area is "land of the covenant" or "land of Israel." In the New Testament, it is usually called Judea, from which the word *Jews* derives.

In the Hebrew Bible, a central teaching about this land is that its only authentic owner is God. In the Torah the divine claim is stressed to the point that the ancient Israelites are themselves seen as foreigners. Says the Lord to Moses on Mount Sinai, "The land shall not be sold in perpetuity, for the land is mine; with me you are but aliens and tenants" (Leviticus 25:23).[1] A concise overview of scriptural sources on the people-land issue appears in the appendix, "Whose Land Is It?"

For Muslims, the "holy" attention has gone mostly to Jerusalem, the city at the heart of this land. In Arabic, the city's name is Al-Quds, which means simply "The Holy." Jerusalem is where, in Islamic understanding, the prophet Muhammad ascended to heaven, from the vicinity of the Dome of the Rock on what Muslims call the Noble Sanctuary and Jews call Temple Mount. For Muslims it stands as the most important shrine after Mecca and Medina.

Indeed, in all three monotheistic faiths, Jerusalem is considered to be a "Holy City." The image appears frequently in the New Testament and has been highly popular in Christian hymnody and poetry.

From Palestine to *Terra Sancta*

The term *Holy Land* is most prominent in Christian usage. It evolved in the time shortly after our Lord Jesus walked those hills and valleys. Christian believers started speaking of Holy Land when the Christian era was quite young. To Latin-speaking Christians in the Roman Empire, it was *Terra Sancta* from early on. This territory, from the time it was a province of the Roman Empire, had the political name Palestine, a Latin term for the Philistines' land. But among Christians the nickname Holy Land became the more popular usage.

Christian leaders of medieval Europe, in promoting the Crusades, argued that "holy land" and "holy places" had to be liberated from non-Christian political control—and that it was God's will for them to do so. The powers who had to be replaced included not just Muslims but also those who, as the Western church saw it, were heretical (Orthodox) Christians. These military enterprises (late eleventh to late thirteenth centuries) had negative results that inflame the passions of many in the Holy Land to this day.

The Ottoman Turks brought Muslim authority to the Holy Land in 1517 (the very year Martin Luther in Europe was launching what became the Reformation). Ottoman rule lasted

Israel and Environs

Map courtesty Foundation for Middle East Peace and Jan de Jong

Israel's Separation Barrier and Settlements in West Bank

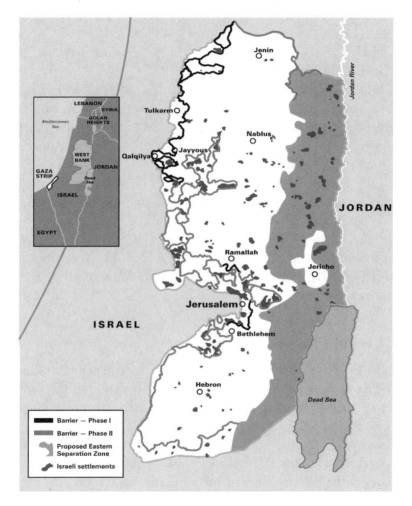

exactly four hundred years, ending in 1917 when the Istanbul-based empire collapsed during World War I. The victorious powers gave governance of the region to the British.

Another political move with religious overtones came in November 1917, when the British government, in the Balfour Declaration, said it viewed "with favour the establishment in Palestine of a national home for the Jewish people." There had always been small communities of Jews living there, but larger numbers of Jews began coming in the two decades between the two world wars.

It is often forgotten, however, that the Balfour Declaration qualified its call for a Jewish homeland with these words: "it being clearly understood that nothing shall be done which may prejudice the civil and religious rights of existing non-Jewish communities in Palestine."

Britain promoted the creation of a Jewish state during the nearly three decades it ruled Palestine under a League of Nations mandate. The United Nations, successor to the league, in November 1947 partitioned the territory into what it intended to be two states. Israel was formally established as a Jewish state in May 1948. An Arab state in the remainder of historic Palestine is yet to be born.

Humans on the Land

The 1947 UN partition plan had 55 percent of Mandate Palestine going to Israel, 45 percent to a Palestinian state. But the Arab neighbors of Israel refused to accept its existence and went to war against the new state. In subsequent fighting, the Israeli share of the land grew to 78 percent, so that the internationally recognized border today (the Green Line of the 1948 ceasefire) has left the Palestinians with just 22 percent of the 1917–47 definition of Palestine. That portion is in the Gaza Strip, the West Bank, and East Jerusalem (see map, page 10).

But even that 22 percent is now further reduced by Israeli settlements with their bypass roads, by Israel's separation wall built inside Palestinian territory, and by Israel's formal annexation of what most of the world community considers Palestinian areas. Subtracting land now on Israel's side of the wall, plus a strip Israel wants to keep along the Jordan Valley, plus East Jerusalem (which Israel claims to have annexed), what remains is calculated to be just 11 percent of Mandate Palestine (see map, p. 11). For Palestinians, this territory would yield a state the size of Rhode Island, with about four times as many people.

Who lives in the Holy Land today? The river-to-sea geography in 2005 was estimated to include a bit more than 10 million people. Israel counts as citizens about 6.5 million. Most Israeli citizens reside within the boundaries of Israel proper, the borders of the state prior to the 1967 war. But more than four hundred thousand Israeli citizens live in settlements within the West Bank and East Jerusalem—land that remains under Israeli occupation nearly four decades after it was taken by military victory in June 1967. Palestinians insist, on various legal and moral grounds, that all this land (the 22 percent) is rightly theirs.

Four-fifths of Israel's total citizenry is Jewish. Nearly all the remaining 20 percent, about 1.3 million people, are Palestinian Arabs. These are non-Jews who lived and stayed in what became Israel in 1948, plus their descendants who still reside as citizens within Israel proper.

Some 3.5 million Palestinians live in the West Bank, Gaza, and East Jerusalem. While most of them aspire to be citizens of a Palestinian state at some future time, at the middle of the first decade in the twenty-first century they remained stateless people. If you add these Palestinians to the 1.3 million who are Israeli citizens, you find that the Holy Land's 10 million divide almost fifty-fifty between those who are Jewish and those who aren't. Given demographic trends, it is expected that within a decade, the non-Jews will have a majority of those living in the land called holy (more on this later in the chapter). Many more Palestinians, probably 4 to 5 million, either live in nearby states (chiefly Jordan and Lebanon) or have emigrated to Western countries. It is likely some would return if a secure, prospering Palestinian state were ever established.

The Shrinking Christian Minority

Christians among the ten million are a tiny minority, one that's in rapid decline as a portion of the total population. Christians were estimated to be about 20 percent of Holy Land population in the early 1900s, and a census during the British Mandate (between the two world wars) put their proportion at 13 percent. In 2005 they numbered only about 1.6 percent. Israel proper has some ninety thousand Christians, living mostly in the Galilean areas of Nazareth and Haifa. The West Bank and East Jerusalem have another seventy thousand, most of these in Bethlehem, Ramallah, East Jerusalem, and nearby communities. During the British Mandate period, when the total population was far smaller, there were more Christians in the Holy Land than there are today.[2]

Three factors contribute to the Christian numerical decline. One is that the natural growth via birthrate is much higher among Muslims. Another is that population growth from in-migration for more than half a century has been heavily Jewish. The third—and most important—reason is that Christians from both Israel and Palestine are leaving proportionately far faster than either Muslims or Jews. Palestinian Christians, often well-educated workers who can't find jobs at home and who have family or professional contacts overseas, have moved out, some to other Middle East countries but most to Europe and North America.

It has been calculated that some three hundred thousand Palestinian Christians are now living abroad, about twice the number who still reside in the Palestinian territories and Israel!

This departure is a matter of profound concern, both to the Christian remnant in the Holy Land and to the Christian community worldwide. Is a time soon coming when the land where Jesus walked will no longer be home to disciples of Jesus? Will the Holy Land be, for touring Christian pilgrims, a kind of biblical theme park with interesting historic sites to see but no living Christians to visit?

Christians as Leavening

And the Christians who leave are precisely the ones who will be most needed, should a just peace ever come to this land. As William Dalrymple has written, a steady emigrant stream of both Christian and Jewish moderates keeps draining both Palestine and Israel, "to escape the rival fanaticisms of the conflict," possibly creating a situation in which only "the fundamentalist [Israeli] settlers [will be] left to confront their opposite numbers in [Palestinian] Hamas." The Christians who leave will be especially missed, says Dalrymple: "The Christian Arabs have always protected the Arab world from the extremes of political Islam. Since the nineteenth century, they have taken a vital part in defining a secular Arab identity. . . . If the Christians continue to emigrate, the Arabs will find it much harder to defend themselves against radical Islamism."[3]

Maintaining Christian presence in the land where Christianity began has political and cultural implications for all people living there, not just for the non-Christian Arabs. Charles Sennott, a secular journalist (longtime *Boston Globe* bureau chief in Jerusalem), in reflecting on the shrinking number of Christians in the Holy Land, puts it this way:

> Important international efforts by Christian churches have been gathering strength to counter the trend of emigration. All of us— Christians, Muslims, and Jews—have a stake in their success. The Christian presence in the Holy Land is a potentially important, possibly essential, voice in the dialogue for peace, but it is a voice that has been reduced to a hoarse whisper. Historically, Christianity has provided a kind of leavening in the Middle East, a small but necessary ingredient acting as a buffer between the Arab world's broad Islamic resurgence and the strands within Israel of a rising ultranationalist brand of Judaism. These two fundamentalist movements, which have fused religion with nationalism, increasingly cast the territorial Israeli-Palestinian conflict in religious

terms. If the Christians disappear, the Middle East will become that much more vulnerable to this embittered dichotomy.[4]

George Hintlian, a Christian and historian living in Jerusalem, has observed that "the churches and the Christian communities are facing an existential threat of the greatest acuteness. Only if, and when, peace comes will the Christians here be able to witness a resurgence as the Christian communities can blend back into their natural environment and rejoin their brethren in the wider Middle East."[5]

Diminishing Global Church Presence

Another kind of Christian presence has been a blessing in that land. It is the strong tradition of international church presence. Much of it maintains humanitarian ministries that make life somewhat more bearable for ordinary people in a conflict situation, for Palestinians particularly. In education and medical care historically—and more recently in ministries of accompaniment among the suffering—this presence by Christians from around the world is of high significance.

But it has come under pressure from Israel's government. During the Second Intifada (2000–5), Israel in three specific ways made life difficult for those in the Holy Land working in the name of the global church:

1. Visas for clergy and other church personnel serving in hospitals, seminaries, congregations, parish schools, and other church institutions have been delayed and denied. The Roman Catholic Church, for example, operates 151 institutions in the Holy Land, with primary staffing by internationals. Protestant denominations have similar institutions. Israeli-created visa problems make it increasingly difficult for international church workers, both paid and volunteer, to gain or maintain a presence.
2. International church agencies have long enjoyed broad tax exemption agreements with the Israeli government. Specifically, Catholic Relief Services, Lutheran World

Federation, and Mennonite Central Committee have for more than fifty years offered services that support the well-being of indigenous people. These humanitarian programs target Palestinians, where the need is greatest, but Israelis have also benefited. In recent years, the Israeli government has sought to cancel the tax exemption agreements for certain charitable institutions that have international support. If upheld by Israel's courts, the taxation change could lead to the closing of programs such as the Lutherans' Augusta Victoria Hospital on the Mount of Olives in Jerusalem.

3. The separation barrier under construction in the Palestinian West Bank is damaging Christian institutions, in many instances separating them from the people they seek to serve. For Christians worldwide who try to visit Christian holy sites, the structure often prohibits access. Speaking of the barrier when it was initially under construction, the Jerusalem bishops and patriarchs said in August 2003, "The consequences will be devastating to the Christian community."

Whether the impact is intentional or not, there is strong evidence that Israeli government policies have harmed the situation and the future of Christianity in the Holy Land.

The Demographic Dilemma

Christians are not the only group that faces declining numerical strength. It is expected that within little more than a decade—present trends continuing—those identifying as Jews within Israel and the occupied territories will be a distinct minority. And that gives Israel what has been called a demographic dilemma.

Demographers predict that, by 2020, of the total population living between the Mediterranean and the Jordan, Jews will number only about 43 percent. The resulting problem for Israel can be illustrated by imagining a three-legged stool, the legs of which are three questions that consume Israeli political discourse:

1. Can occupied territories (West Bank, Gaza, East Jerusalem)
   be annexed into Israel proper?
2. Can Israel remain a democracy?
3. Can Israel remain a Jewish (majority) state?

This stool has trouble standing because only two of its three legs can be together at one time—never all three. That is, the occupied territories could be incorporated into the state of Israel with democracy open equally to all, including the Palestinians, but Israel would no longer be a state with a Jewish majority. Or Israel could remain a Jewish state and a democracy but forget about absorbing the Palestinian West Bank, East Jerusalem, and Gaza. Lastly, Israel could remain a Jewish state *and* absorb the occupied territories but not give their Palestinian residents citizenship in a democratic society. This last possibility, in fact, is pretty close to what Palestinians have lived with for nearly four decades of Israeli occupation.

What strikes many observers about recent Israeli government behavior is that it is pursuing a strategy of incorporating into Israel the Palestinian *land* without the Palestinian *people*. That is, by various means, Israel's government policies seem to promote the departure and exclusion of Palestinians from Palestinian territory.

Many Palestinians have found daily existence to be no longer endurable. A combination of factors—increasing harassment from Israeli settler-neighbors, erection of the barrier dividing Palestinians from Palestinians, horrible economic realities (unemployment at 60 percent), and the daily humiliation of living as prisoners in their own land under an occupying army—have led many Palestinians to emigrate. They have left for other Middle East locales or for the West. Those leaving are, disproportionately, Christians.

Christian Incarnation Theology

Of course, this land is important to those who live and die there. But why should it matter much to people who live and die halfway around the planet? I see two reasons. The first is specifically for Christians; it comes out of both Christian theology and Christian experience.

Generations of Christians have become attached to this bit of geography from earliest childhood. It has been at the heart of our very nurturing in the faith. It is the locus for all those Bible stories we first heard as little ones. It is in the maps we paged to at the backs of our Bibles and saw hanging in our Sunday school rooms. It was in our mind's eye as we sang hymns and heard lessons read in Sunday liturgy and listened to preachers tell us about Jesus' earthly life and healing work and death and resurrection on our behalf.

Yes, we learned that all of God's creation is sacred and that no one space on earth is holier than any other. But we also learned that Christians understand God as One who entered into human history and geography in a unique way—at a particular *time*, in a particular *place*. We learned that Jesus was born of an identified historic woman, with a distinct ethnicity, among a people living under a specific imperial occupation, and that he died on a cross on the outskirts of a living human community.

What shall we make of all this? We say there is Christian logic to giving special place in our devotion to Mary and Joseph. It is just as logical to have special regard for the earthly space into which our Lord came. Christians have an incarnation theology: our God comes to be with us in the flesh, in human form. Part of incarnation theology is to recognize that he came, born of Mary, born as a Jew, in a most definite time and place. And that place is the space long named Holy Land.

Naim Ateek, a Palestinian Christian scholar, says Christian thought about the land always moves between the universal and the particular:

> The dimensions of the gospel have shattered the geographic focus on the land of Palestine. God's love for the world in Christ encompassed all people. . . . [But] later in the life of the church the [Holy] land started again assuming greater significance . . . for the

church, because the church lives in history and because God in Christ had taken history very seriously. And Christians from early centuries made pilgrimage to the land, because the land hosted the Holy One.[6]

Land Now Is Secularized

Yes, for Christians the gospel has indeed "shattered the geographic focus," our preoccupation with this land. Any special religious meaning for the land called holy is, for New Testament people, significantly qualified. In Christ, there is a universalizing of God's love, extending it to Gentiles as well as Jews. In Christ, all lands become equally holy.

Or, as Dr. Philip Quanbeck has put it, "In Christ there is a secularization of both space and time. Any time, even the Sabbath, can be used for doing good works. And any place can be sacred if it is a place where we meet God." In John's Gospel, Jesus reminds us that we are to worship God at no set-aside holy spot: "neither on this mountain nor in Jerusalem . . . [but] in spirit and truth" (John 4:21, 23).

In fact, it is probably true that both of today's Holy Land peoples, Jews and Palestinians, think too much about land and not enough about people. What is important is not the land itself, but seeking justice for people who, in order to live, must have access to land and its resources. The land is thus a means to the end of securing justice and peace.

Not a Fairyland

So we do not worship that land. It has no sacred character that we deny to other parts of the creation. Yet in our devotional life, it has a spot of special reverence given to nowhere else. Donald Bridge says it well:

There is nothing mythical about the Holy Land. The rocks are solid, the sand is gritty, the water is wet. Nazareth is not in fairyland; it is perched on the stony hills beside the Jezreel valley. Bethlehem is not a scene conjured up for Christmas cards; it is a town

on the edge of the Judaean hills. . . . You cannot take a taxi or climb
off a bus or go for a stroll . . . without stopping at some physical
spot and saying in wonder, "God did this HERE . . . it happened
HERE." This is vital. Not because the places carry some aura of
holiness or grace, but because our faith depends on things that
God said and did in particular places at a particular time. The
gospel is . . . about things that really happened. . . . The Christian
faith, and indeed the Jewish faith, is committed to fact. God is
known by what God is seen to have done.[7]

So it should be clear: this land has special hold on the intel-
lect and the emotions of Christian believers, because this is
where God entered most dramatically, most concretely, into the
human story. This is where God acted, in history, creating (as
politicians in that land still like to say) "facts on the ground."[8]

A Flesh/Land Incarnation

Biblical scholars have noted that the "fullness of time" (Ephesians
1:10) in which Jesus came to earth was accompanied by a "fullness of space." That is, Rome's Palestinian province was a most
fitting locale in which God should enter human history as God
did. God had chosen the Jews as the bearers of God's Messiah,
and Palestine is where the Jews were. But Palestine was also
geographically well suited to play host to God's peculiar mission. So we can say that God had chosen not just a people. That
choice means God also chose a land.

Palestine, Judea, Land of Israel—whatever we wish to
call it—had no political power two thousand years ago. Yet
all through human history, that land has held a central position among the earthly powers. The routes of trade and culture led through it. Indeed, the prophet Isaiah, seven centuries
before Christ, envisioned a time when the land of Israel would
be a bridge of blessing, linking the powers of Egypt and Assyria
(which is essentially modern Syria and Iraq) in a kind of faith-
peace triple alliance:

On that day there will be a highway from Egypt to Assyria . . . and the Egyptians will worship with the Assyrians. On that day Israel will be the third with Egypt and Assyria, a blessing in the midst of the earth, whom the Lord of hosts has blessed, saying, "Blessed be Egypt my people, and Assyria the work of my hands, and Israel my heritage." (Isaiah 19:23–25)

In the time of Jesus and the early church, because this land was part of the empire called Rome, it was well situated as the base for evangelizing outreach to most of the known world. The rapid spread of Christianity under Paul and others would soon make that evident.

So we have an incarnation theology of both flesh and land. What does it say to those who today make pilgrimage to the Holy Land? Some pilgrims think they must seek the very paths that Jesus trod, sit on the stones where he sat, and soak in the water with which he was baptized. As though that were possible!

The Christians living there today like to remind us that the physical elements of the landscape, while poetically and aesthetically enticing, have little significance for connecting us with a vital faith. What is most important for Christians who visit the Holy Land today is to engage with the believers who live there today. These living stones of the land where Jesus walked are the ones we need to meet and learn from and pray with and support.

A Matter of Justice

And that leads to my second chief reason for Christians world-wide to give attention to the Holy Land. I think it clearly is the place in today's world that is most starved of justice and peace. It's a starvation that has tragically negative effects on the well-being of the entire earthly community. It is not the land, finally, but *people* who are crying out for justice.

Christians everywhere in the world have a call from God to work for justice and peace anywhere in the world. And Christians in the United States, because we are citizens of Planet Earth's sole superpower, need especially to heed God's call to "seek peace and pursue it" (Psalm 34:14).

Christian pilgrimage to the Holy Land has been seriously diminished by that region's violence in recent years. What tourism does remain is profoundly shaped by the politics of the Israeli-Palestinian conflict. Our public-policy advocacy and our support for ministries of local Christians must also be addressed in the context of Holy Land political realities, of course. All these matters are discussed in more detail later (mainly chapter 4).

Not Just Land

When we speak of justice for the people of the Holy Land, it's not just land we're talking about. At least as important as the right to land (some say more important) is the right to water. In a region that's semiarid at best and often plagued by drought, which of two peoples will have access to which water sources—and who will decide? Since 1967, the Israelis decide how much water the Palestinians may have and at what cost.

There is surface water available to this land, in the Sea of Galilee and the Jordan River. But these waters, via a 1996 treaty, are divided between the state of Israel and the kingdom of Jordan. Palestinians who live on the Jordan River's West Bank don't get a drop of Jordan River water. The only permanent source of water for Palestinians is underground, in West Bank aquifers. In Gaza, the underground water is easy to pump but contaminated increasingly by seawater and untreated sewage.

The water lying below Israel and the West Bank is of good quality but is quite deep and thus costly to pump. Of the aquifers located chiefly below Israel, 100 percent is taken by Israel. Of those under the West Bank, Palestinians get 20 percent, Israelis 80 percent. It is well documented that a typical Israeli each year uses four times the amount of water granted to the average Palestinian.

The illegal Israeli settlements on West Bank land and the construction of the separation barrier inside Palestinian territory steal not just Palestinian land. They also take water away from Palestinians. One result of this "water war," writes Mark Zeitoun, is a marketplace injustice that is particularly offensive:

> Private (Palestinian) water-tankers lumber up to the settlements . . . looking for water to take back to villagers who are immobile in their sealed-off villages—and thirsty. At a price between five and 15 times that charged by the Israeli government, there is always a settler willing to make the deal. The irony of this lucrative, illegal business is not lost on the Palestinian farmer. Not only is the water "stolen" from under his feet, he is then actually forced to buy it back from the "thief."[9]

One Person's Journey

Before we go further into current matters of Holy Land justice and peace, the reader deserves to know the writer's personal story on a matter as charged as this one. So I give you a quick overview of a six-decade-long evolution.

I was in my early teens, with a father serving as chaplain to U.S. forces fighting the Nazis, when I first learned that huge numbers of Jews had died under the Germans led by Adolf Hitler. A few years later, in 1947, I was a high school kid in Iowa who was pleased to learn that the United Nations had declared a partition of British Mandate Palestine into one region that should be a state for Jews and another to become a state for Palestinians. As did most Americans, I saw it as a just response by the world community to the horrible tragedy of the Holocaust.

Over the next few decades, I lamented that the Arab peoples of the Middle East refused to accept the state of Israel as a fact. And I wondered if there would ever be peace between the Arabs and the Israelis. I rejoiced with U.S. Jewish friends when Israel won military victories in 1967 and 1973. But then I wondered whether Israel should insist on staying as an occupier in Palestinian lands.

God Wants an Expanded Israel?

After these war victories and the subsequent military occupations, it seemed that a new political theology had taken over in
Israel. Whereas the founding Zionist vision was basically secular, since 1967 the policies of Israeli governments have increasingly found rootage in divine authorization.

Language from the Hebrew scriptures was borrowed to des-
ignate Palestinian lands occupied by Israel. It wasn't the "West
Bank" or "Palestine" that Israel occupied; it was now "Judea and
Samaria." And the clear implication was that no less a power
than God supported Israeli expansionism. Religious ideology
became a primary motivator for the settlement policy. It justified, contrary to international law, the moving of several hundred thousand Israelis permanently onto Palestinian land that
was occupied by Israel's military.

Moshe Dayan, military hero of the 1967 war, in August
1967 gave resounding expression to this new Israeli vision of
returning Jews to all the lands of their Israelite ancestors. Dayan
was speaking at a ceremony on the Mount of Olives, located in
Arab East Jerusalem. Religious Jews view the mount as a preferred burial site because tradition says the Messiah will arrive
there. (Burial geography is often a politically potent symbol, as
we were reminded in late 2004 by the very public dispute over
Yasser Arafat's final resting place.)

In 1967, with Israel newly in control of the Mount of Olives,
the government decided to rebury there the bodies of soldiers
who had died in the 1948 independence struggle. At the reburial
ceremony, Dayan said:

> Our brothers, who fought in the war of Independence: we have not
> abandoned your dream, nor forgotten the lesson you taught us. . . .
> We have returned to the Mount, to the cradle of this nation's his-
> tory, to the land of our forefathers, to the land of the Judges, and
> to the fortress of David's dynasty. We have returned to Hebron,
> Shechem, Bethlehem . . . to Jericho and the ford over the Jordan.
> Our brothers, we bear your lessons with us . . . we know that to

give life to Jerusalem we must station the soldiers and armour of
the Israeli Defense Forces on the Shechem mountains and on the
bridges over the Jordan.[10]

Kahane in Israel Lives On

In late 1969, a visitor came to see me at work in the U.S. office
of the World Council of Churches in New York City. One of
my tasks as a second-level staffer was to handle Jewish-Christian
relations for the WCC in the United States. So the visitor was
directed to my desk. He was a young Jewish rabbi from Brooklyn
named Meir Kahane and said he represented a group called the
Jewish Defense League.

Rabbi Kahane told me he wanted the World Council of
Churches publicly to declare support for the position that *all*
of historic Palestine, from the Mediterranean Sea to the Jordan
River, had been given by God forever to the Jews. I told the
rabbi that, while some conservative Christians might hold such
a view, I believed there was no way the churches of the WCC
would endorse that position.

Kahane moved to Israel in 1974 and ten years later was
elected to the Knesset (Israel's parliament). He and his party,
Kach, pressed for a policy of removing all Palestinians from
both Israel proper and the occupied territories. The rabbi was
killed at a New York City hotel while on a visit in 1990. (An
Arab named El Sayyid Nosair was charged with his murder but
acquitted; in 1996 he was sentenced to life in prison for his role
in plans to bomb New York City sites, including the World
Trade Center attack in 1993.)

Kahane's political party was banned from civic participation
by Israel in 1994, and later the U.S. State Department labeled
it a terrorist organization. Itamar is today a Jewish settlement of
some one thousand Kahane followers, south and east of Nablus
in the West Bank, near the Palestinian village of Yanoun. The
Itamar settlers have built outposts surrounding Yanoun, indicating their intention of driving the villagers out completely and

forever. In the year 2005, one could still spot bumper stickers on Israeli autos proclaiming, "Rabbi Kahane lives," or "Kahane was right."

Personal Visits

In 1979 I was joyful when a peace agreement was reached between the leaders of Israel and Egypt, its most powerful Arab neighbor, at Camp David under President Jimmy Carter. And I looked longingly, with most of the world, for the completion of that agreement's other promise, the creation of an independent Palestinian state alongside Israel. Now, more than a quarter century later, an independent Palestine has the support of another U.S. president, and its establishment may be possible.

My first of many visits to the Holy Land came in 1982, when Israel's military was occupying not only the Palestinian territories and the Golan Heights in Syria, but also a slice of southern Lebanon. On that trip we had an Israeli guide, an officer in Israel's air force reserve. He did an acceptable job of explaining the significance of biblical sites but gave a clearly one-sided interpretation of current political realities. Our group debriefed each evening, and our group leaders, Americans who had worked several years at the YMCA in Nazareth, offered a more Palestinian-oriented interpretation of that day's experience.

That two-week experience was my first systematic exposure to the fact that two peoples with overlapping histories have two quite different stories to tell. The 1982 visit was also my first chance to meet with Holy Land Christians, both Israelis and Palestinians. In the years since, I've been privileged to meet and to know many more of them. I've also had opportunity to see firsthand the humanitarian work that the global church community sustains, and how vital it is to life itself for the many Palestinians existing at high risk. A 1991 visit focused on the work of the world's Lutheran community in health and education among the Palestinians, and I have followed those ministries in all subsequent visits.

Oslo: Hope and Hopelessness

I rejoiced when the Oslo Accords were announced in 1993 under
the guidance of another American president, Bill Clinton, and
then despaired as those promises turned to garbage by the close
of his presidency. While with a group visiting the Holy Land in
spring 1997, I heard words of deep cynicism from Palestinians
(as well as Israeli peace activists). They said Israel's launch of a
huge new settlement on Har Homa, Palestinian-claimed land
and the last open hillside between Jerusalem and Bethlehem,
proved that Israel's government had no interest in peace and
that Oslo was dead.

By the time of my next visit, the fall of 1999, there was even
more despair about the chances of a just peace. Then, in the last
days of the Clinton administration, at Camp David in summer
2000 and even into January 2001 at Taba in the Sinai, U.S.-
sponsored efforts sought to reach a resolution of the conflict.
Just then, the second Palestinian intifada (uprising) was gaining
steam. It was surely birthed by Palestinian frustration at living
still under military occupation after being promised a new day
that was clearly not coming. In 2000, economic conditions and
daily life were much worse for Palestinians than they had been
seven years earlier, providing a fertile seedbed for frustration
and the Al-Aqsa Intifada.

Then in 2003 we entered the period of the Bush road map, a
peace proposal endorsed by "the Quartet"—the United Nations,
European Union, and Russia along with the United States. In
2003, a U.S. president again committed himself to seeking a just
peace between the two Holy Land parties, with the stated objec-
tive of an end to violence and two independent states coexisting
in mutual respect.

But again a so-called peace process floundered. It can be
charged that both sides in the conflict have failed to abide by
up-front conditions required by the road map: Palestinian
militants ending violence against civilian Israelis; Israel's government ending settlement expansion and daily oppression
of civilian Palestinians. The separation barrier built by Israel

inside Palestinian territory provided the most visible symbol of the road map's demise.

The fault lay not only with Israelis and Palestinians. As his attention shifted elsewhere, President Bush's bold rhetoric supporting the creation of a Palestinian state was abandoned for two years. And the matter of Israel and Palestine was almost entirely ignored by both sides during the 2004 U.S. presidential campaign. Then, after the death of Yasser Arafat and the election (early 2005) of a new Palestinian leader, Mahmoud Abbas (Abu Mazen), the Palestine-Israel peace prospect returned to the front burner. Both President George W. Bush and Prime Minister Ariel Sharon have had meetings with President Abbas (both had refused to meet with Arafat). So 2005 brought new hope of a negotiated resolution of this long conflict.

I joined many in hoping that the new shape of the situation would finally produce a peaceful and secure reality for two peoples to live together, side by side in two states. And after the Israeli withdrawal of 8,500 settlers from Gaza in August 2005, I joined those who expressed the hope that it was a matter of "Gaza first, not Gaza last." There were two underlying questions surrounding the Gaza withdrawal: Would it lead to true independence from Israeli control for the 1.3 million Palestinians living in Gaza, or would they exist in a large, open-air prison with all access of goods and people to and from Gaza dependent on Israel's permission? Further, would withdrawal of the illegal settlements in Gaza be followed by action on the equally unlawful (in international understanding) settlements in the West Bank and East Jerusalem. It is widely assumed that decisions about the non-Gaza settlers, who number some 450,000, will have to come via negotiations between Palestinians and Israelis. Will negotiators ever get to the negotiating table? At this writing (late 2005), they had not.

Relations with U.S. Jews

Part of my personal history on the Palestinian-Israeli conflict concerns the matter of relating to American Jews. I confess to a feeling of some responsibility for what Jews have suffered historically at the hands of Western Christians. While I did not personally take part in persecution of any sort—in Europe or North America or anywhere else—I do identify as a Lutheran of German heritage. And I know that perpetrators of the Holocaust in Hitler's Germany used the virulently anti-Jewish writings of Martin Luther to help justify their deeds of annihilation.

I abhor the Luther who, because Jews would not convert to Christianity, condemned them, urging a boycott of their businesses and a burning of their synagogues and schools. Such venom has no place in the Christian faith, and those writings from Luther have been denounced by Lutheran churches worldwide. Still, there is a nagging sense that at least some of the people who were my people in Germany six and seven decades ago did not stand with Jewish people against the Nazi demons when they should have.

There is a fairly widespread feeling of Holocaust guilt among Christians in the United States to the present day. Indeed, it may be most pronounced among German-Americans who identify as Lutherans. For me, it's always lurking in the background when I relate to American Jews. It seems to surface particularly when the agenda is the state of Israel or the Israeli-Palestinian conflict.

One result of this guilt is that, with many other Christians, I feel some reluctance to criticize the behavior and policies of the Israeli government. Another result is that, as many observers have noted, it is the Palestinians who now are paying for centuries of sinning by Western Christians against the Jews.

When Anti-Israel Is Anti-Jewish

Clearly, there are times when some American Jews brand any criticism of Israel as anti-Semitic ("anti-Jewish" is a better term, since both Arabs and Jews are Semitic peoples). In my own experience, not many Jews have taken this approach. But those who do are typically official spokespersons for U.S.

Jewish organizations, both synagogues and public-policy lobbying groups. They know well how to play the Holocaust-guilt card with Christians who speak critically of Israel.[11]

Is it automatically, inevitably anti-Jewish (anti-Semitic) to be critical of Israeli government policies and practices? No, but it may be and sometimes is. Natan Sharansky, a Russian Jew who spent some years as a member of the Israeli cabinet, provides a helpful guideline:

> I offer a simple "3-D" test for differentiating legitimate criticism of Israel from antisemitism. . . . The first "D" is the test of demonization . . . depicting modern-day Israel as the embodiment of evil. The second "D" is the test of double standards. . . . In other words, do similar policies pursued by other governments produce similar criticism? . . . The third "D" is the test of delegitimization. . . . While criticism of an Israeli policy may not be antisemitic, the denial of Israel's right to exist is always antisemitic.[12]

I have come to know a large number of American Jews who vocally oppose the Israeli government's continuing control of Palestinians. They lament the fact that their beloved Israel, created as a haven for people who had suffered millennia of oppression, has now become itself an oppressor of others. They want the occupation of Palestinian lands and oppression of Palestinian people ended, and they want the settlers to go home, back to Israel. When speaking thus, they must endure fellow Jews—those who believe the state of Israel can do no wrong and is above criticism—denouncing them as "self-hating Jews."

The bottom line of this issue is that the Christian-Jewish relationship labors under serious stress whenever the Palestinian-Israeli relationship is on the agenda. American Jews must, I believe, see that Christians can criticize Israeli policies without being branded as systematically anti-Jewish. And U.S. Christians need to keep showing their respect and love for Jews, even as we challenge policies and behaviors of Israel's government.

Also in Abraham's Tent

And what of the Christian-Muslim relationship? It is obvious that Muslims see Palestine as essentially part of the Muslim world. And for nearly all of that world, the liberation of occupied Palestine from Israeli oppression is a central concern.

When Muslims talk about the land called holy in religious terms, they typically remind everyone that the promise to Abraham includes more than Jews. Today's Arabs are also Abraham's heirs.[13] And the faith traditions tracing themselves back to Father Abraham include Jews, Christians, and Muslims.

Most Muslims in North America, particularly those of Arab origin, put resolution of the Israeli-Palestinian conflict at the very top of their list of global policy objectives. When Muslims in the United States engage these days in dialogue with Christians, the agenda brought by Muslims always includes two questions:

1. What are we Christians saying to the U.S. government about its failure to be evenhanded in seeking a just peace between Israel and Palestine?
2. What are we saying to the government about its profiling of Muslims and frequent curtailment of their civil rights since the attacks of September 11, 2001?

U.S. Muslims say they rarely have opportunity even to pose these questions to the Christian Right in America, since almost no dialogue is going on. But they do yearn for such conversation with Christians who are politically and theologically more moderate.

Where God Suffers

Dietrich Bonhoeffer, the German Lutheran who was martyred under Hitler, said that a Christian is one who shares the suffering of God in the world—"watching with Christ in Gethsemane."[14] Sadly, the case can be made that there is no place in the world where God's suffering is deeper or of longer duration than in the land surrounding Gethsemane, the land to which God's Son came and where he suffered, this land we still name, in somewhat awkward embarrassment, Holy.

So do Christians have a special obligation regarding the Holy Land? The leaders of the indigenous churches believe so. This is what the Roman Catholic, Episcopal, and Lutheran bishops of the Holy Land said in their Easter 2005 "Call from Jerusalem" to church leaders around the planet:

> We believe that the churches can and must do more to recognize their duty towards the Holy Land and act together to sensitize their governments, their people, and the international community. Our communities ask your help so that justice will prevail and so that Palestinian Christians will flourish in the Holy Land and be strengthened to carry out our mission in the power of the Resurrection.[15]

Further, many have argued that, since forgiveness is such a central theme in Christianity, Christians must lead the way in the teaching and practice of forgiveness that will be an essential part of a just peace. Israelis and Palestinians, Jews, Muslims, and Christians—all will need to learn the art of forgiveness, and much will need to be forgiven.

Finally, the one place in the world beyond the Holy Land where theological and political convictions about that land are most impassioned, most heated, most deeply felt surely appears to be the United States of America. What does this all mean for U.S. Christians? What is expected of Christ's followers today, as we join God in the suffering? The rest of this book seeks to respond to those questions.

Redeemer Lutheran Church, Old City, Jerusalem. This church houses the offices of Palestinian Lutheran Bishop Munib Younan.

Chapter 2

Politics, Faiths, and Fundamentalisms

Robert O. Smith

Christian appeal to biblical land traditions must insist that land possession is held, according to that tradition, only as land practices are under the discipline of neighbor practices grounded in the Torah. Any claim of land apart from that Torah tradition is deeply suspect and open to profound critique.

Walter Brueggemann, in *The Land: Place as Gift, Promise, and Challenge in Biblical Faith*

In February 2002, the Reverend Munib Younan, bishop of the Evangelical Lutheran Church in Jordan and the Holy Land (ELCJHL),[1] was scheduled to visit my school, Luther Seminary in Saint Paul, Minnesota. Almost a celebrity in my mind, Bishop Younan was coming as a witness from Jerusalem, bringing the word of the Lord from all Judea and Samaria to the ends of the earth (Acts 1:8). I was surprised, then, when my friend Reem asked me to lead worship with Bishop Younan in our seminary's daily chapel service. Reem is a Palestinian refugee, born in Bethlehem.

Through our friendship, Reem and I have had many conversations about her feelings for the land of her birth, the land where Jesus walked, the land that embodied her heritage as a Palestinian Christian. As the only Palestinian or Arab then on our midwinter Minnesota campus, Reem had been asked to lead worship with Bishop Younan, but she was worried: "I'm afraid I'll be too emotional to get through the prayers that need to be said," she said.

I accepted in her stead but asked if she would like a hand in putting the prayers in order, so they would express what needed to be said. "No, I don't think that will be necessary," Reem responded. "I trust you."

Over the next few days, I chose the hymns, decided the order of the liturgy, and prepared the prayers, including an opening litany based on one that Bishop Younan had delivered the year before in Jerusalem. As we led worship together, a fourth-year seminarian and the bishop of one of the smallest yet most prominent Lutheran communities in the world, I caught a glimpse of Reem, sitting stoic, proud that her people were being honored that cold Minnesota morning.

Later, I learned that, for Reem, Bishop Younan was more than a visiting dignitary. He had been the principal of Reem's school, and even though she was Greek Orthodox, she approached him as her father. I had been included in this web of relationships. In humble acts of service—in education, in leading our community's worship, in lifting our brothers and sisters in prayer—we are bound together in faithful solidarity.

To stand in solidarity with Reem is to appreciate her attachment to the land she calls home. Her storied space—her home—is a place of soil and family, not some ethereal Holy Land. But as she understands it, her home has been taken from her. She has been forced out, threatened with never being able to return, even if only to visit. This storied place—filled with stories of family, not just the biblical or historical stories outsiders might tell—has been closed off for Reem and for so many others.

Still, the land calls. It calls Reem as a Christian. It calls her as a Palestinian. But she understands that it calls other people as well. The land calls Muslims, whether they are Palestinian or not. And it calls Jews, whether or not they hope one day to live in the land. How can American Christians respond to the competing claims these communities have to this storied place and the violence too often engendered by those competing claims? Are we, both as individuals and as a community, also called by this place?

Where Land Is More than Land

As any farmer or rancher will attest, "land" is more than the dirt under one's feet. To question a farmer's claim to land is to challenge the very soil of his or her life. Land carries many meanings and values: land is soil and production, but it is also proper *place*, it is identity, it is nation. By itself, and not just for farmers, "land" is almost sacred.

So it is with the land of Israel/Palestine,[2] where centuries of tradition in many communities—including Jews, Christians, and Muslims—imbue the land with shades of meaning. This chapter on the interrelations of religion, land, and violence takes a critical look at how North American Christians might more responsibly join in solidarity with both Jews *and* Palestinians as all seek to be peacemakers in twenty-first-century Israel/Palestine.

In North America—where land is most often a commodity for individuals and corporations to possess, buy, and sell—it can be difficult to comprehend the depth of conflict surrounding the land of Israel/Palestine. Our understanding of religion itself further complicates this conversation. We have inherited a view of religions that perceives them as clusters of abstracted doctrine, an approach that assumes religion is essentially place-less. In truth, however, every religion is profoundly located, grounded in certain places and times.

While the three Abrahamic religions—Judaism, Christianity, and Islam—do not rely solely on topographical specificity, the land still forms a significant component of each community's meaning and faith. Since struggles between the state of Israel and its Palestinian population (both internal and external) are deeply affected by the double helix of land and identity, even relatively mundane topics like urban planning, security, and water rights can become infused with ultimate concern. Neither merely political nor merely theological, the matters discussed in this chapter and the next therefore are properly called theopolitical. (For a brief summary of the Holy Land thinking of current Christian scholars, see the appendix, "Whose Land Is It?" by Ronald D. Witherup.)

Judaism

Of the three faiths, Judaism has in our time come to be identified most closely with Israel/Palestine. This perception has been fortified by the modern state of Israel. As biblical scholar Walter Brueggemann has said, "It is clear that, since the recent wars of the state of Israel, Christians cannot speak seriously to Jews unless we acknowledge land to be the central agenda."[3]

In *Essential Judaism*, George Robinson knots the narrative thread that runs through the Tanakh (what Christians generally refer to as the Old Testament): "The biblical history of the Jews consists of a series of covenants made by God with Adam, Noah, Abraham, Jacob, Moses, David, followed by transgressions of humanity resulting in expulsions by God and periods of exile, leading eventually to some sort of redemption and God's forgiveness."[4] The central element of these covenants is the gift of land to descendants of Israel, called by God to be a blessing to all nations.

While Jewish approaches to the Land of Israel (*Eretz Yisrael* in Hebrew) are complex and varied, the land has long been the central pole to which the children of Abraham, Isaac, and Jacob are tethered. However, the geographic area of the land promised to the patriarchs is unclear. Most biblical descriptions have it stretching from the southern desert of modern Israel to Lebanon and from the Mediterranean to the Euphrates River, located in modern Iraq (Exodus 23:31; Deuteronomy 11:24; Joshua 1:4). Genesis 15:18 expands the area westward to the Nile. While some apologists for the modern state of Israel argue for a policy of expanding into a "Greater Israel" that encompasses the maximum acreage mentioned in the Bible, most are content to accept the borders of the present state. The contentious point of debate is whether the present state is understood to include the West Bank, East Jerusalem, and Gaza.[5]

The covenant of land is established and reestablished throughout the Torah. When, for instance, Abram (to be renamed Abraham) first sojourns through Canaan, God appears to him with this promise: "I will make of you a great nation, and I will bless you, and make your name great, so that you will be a blessing. . . . To your offspring I will give this land" (Genesis 12:2, 7). The promise is repeated to Jacob when he is renamed Israel (Genesis 35:9-12) and then again to Moses (Exodus 6:2-5).

Throughout their journey to the land, the people are constantly reminded that they have been constituted by God and their hope is in God alone (Leviticus 25:38). But God also needs to be reminded of the covenant, to quell God's wrath in response to his children's rebellion (Exodus 32:13-14). Finally, as the people reach the precipice of the promised land, the covenant and its history are once again placed before the people: "See, I have set the land before you; go in and take possession of the land that I swore to your ancestors, to Abraham, to Isaac, and to Jacob, to give to them and to their descendants after them" (Deuteronomy 1:8).

The dynamic relationship between God and the Children of Israel—including frequent covenantal reminders—has been perpetuated throughout the centuries. Yet, though the promises made to Abram and extended to Israel were unequivocal, they were made within a reciprocal, covenantal relationship:

Keep, then, this entire commandment that I am commanding you today, so that you may have strength to go in and occupy the land that you are crossing over to occupy, and so that you may live long in the land that the LORD swore to your ancestors to give them and to their descendants, a land flowing with milk and honey. (Deuteronomy 11:8-9; see also 19:8-9, 28:7-12)[6]

Covenant: Eternal and Conditional

Although the covenant is eternal—it can be neither abrogated nor superseded—it is conditional. The benefits of God's covenant with the Children of Israel are enjoyed according to the moral and ritual obligations of the Torah, given via God's steadfast grace.

So the people of God might "live long in the land," the regulations of the Torah are quite specific. God's commandments, concerned first with how the Jewish community treats its own people, contain several injunctions for the proper treatment of others outside the community, even those aliens and outsiders with whom Jews are in conflict: "If you besiege a town for a long time, making war against it in order to take it, you must not destroy its trees by wielding an ax against them. Although you may take food from them, you must not cut them down. Are trees in the field human beings that they should come under siege from you?" (Deuteronomy 20:19). Commenting on this commandment, the famous medieval Jewish philosopher and theologian Maimonides expanded the prohibition: "Not only one who cuts down a fruit tree, but anyone who destroys household goods, tears clothing, demolishes a building, stops up a spring, or ruins food deliberately, violates the prohibition *bal tashhit*, 'you must not destroy.'"[7] Further commandments include not moving "a neighbor's boundary marker" and not depriving "the alien, the orphan, and the widow of justice" (Deuteronomy 27:17, 19).

Deuteronomy is not alone in insisting that the covenant of land is conditioned upon acts of justice being done by the Children of Israel. In Exodus, we find this injunction from God: "You shall not wrong or oppress a resident alien, for you were aliens in the land of Egypt" (22:21). The prophets seized upon the covenant's conditionality as a possible explanation for the Babylonian exile and the destruction of Solomon's Temple (as well as the preceding political and religious collapse). Jeremiah, for instance, records God's lament: "I thought how I would set you among my children, and give you a pleasant land, the most beautiful heritage of all the nations. And I thought you would call me, My Father, and would not turn from following me. Instead, as a faithless wife leaves her husband, so you have been faithless to me, O house of Israel, says the LORD" (3:19-20). A similar lament is found in Ezekiel 20.

Later in Ezekiel (47:21-23), the hope of the land is again held out to the Children of Israel as the end of exile is envisioned. There, one again notices the conspicuous presence of "aliens" among the "citizens of Israel" and the concern God voices for them, even in the direst of circumstances.

And Jerusalem?

The city of Jerusalem is the hub around which traditional Jewish concern for the land revolves.[8] David captured the city (roughly 1000 BCE) and made it the capital of his kingdom. While David wished to build a temple there, God advised him that this job would be entrusted to his son, Solomon. Through the Davidic line, then, "The LORD, the God of Israel, has given rest to his people; and he resides in Jerusalem forever" (1 Chronicles 23:25). The Temple was soon established as the dwelling place of God.[9] The importance of Jerusalem and Zion, the holy hill on which the Temple was established, began to flavor the writings now collected in the Hebrew Bible. References to Jerusalem, often personified as a beautiful young woman, fill the Psalms.

But Jerusalem failed as the expected stronghold of God's authority against earthly power. In 586 BCE, the Temple was destroyed when the Babylonians captured the city. The prophets struggled to make sense of this new situation of exile. Beyond theological concerns, the Jewish concept of land was now presented with a political problem: "From then on, except for a short period under the Hasmoneans . . . , Jerusalem and the area around the city came under the control of one foreign power or another."[10] The Herods, under Roman rule, rebuilt the Temple from 19 BCE to 64 CE, only to have it destroyed by the Romans in 70.

Beyond mere theological or political considerations, the destruction of the Second Temple and the military defeats of 70 and 135 CE radically changed the practical expression of Jewish faith. Jewish practice shifted to the home, and community leadership was concentrated in the synagogues, inaugurating what has been called a new era in Judaism.[11]

Nevertheless, these words from Psalm 137 still ring down through the ages of Jewish tradition: "If I forget you, O Jerusalem, let my right hand wither! Let my tongue cling to the roof of my mouth, if I do not remember you, if I do not set Jerusalem above my highest joy" (vv. 5-6). Many Jews still observe *Tisha b'Av* (the ninth of the Jewish month of Av), a day of sorrowful fasting commemorating the destruction of the First and Second Temples.[12] Every year, the Seder celebrated at *Pesach* (Passover) ends with the acclamation, "Next year in Jerusalem."[13]

Christianity

Most contemporary expressions of global Christianity have been divorced from the religion's original Palestinian context. Historian and biblical scholar W. D. Davies characterized the typical Christian approach to the land in this way: "Like everything else, the land also in the New Testament drives us to ponder the mystery of Jesus, the Christ, who by his cross and resurrection broke not only the bonds of death for early Christians, but also the bonds of the land." Today, most North American Christians are more likely to identify their faith traditions with European locales than with Palestine: Lutherans have a special fondness for Germany and Scandinavia, Calvinists for Geneva and the Netherlands, Roman Catholics for the Vatican, Episcopalians for London. Davies's characterization of the early Christian community holds for their contemporaries: "The people of Israel living in the land had been replaced as the people of God by a universal community which had no special territorial attachment."[14]

The fact of history, however, is that Christianity was first a Middle Eastern religion and that Jesus, the object of its discipleship, was a Palestinian Jew. Neglecting the historical particularity of Christian faith has ethical implications. In a post-Holocaust era, for instance, alarms sound when Christians speak of Jews being "replaced as the people of God." According to Franklin Littell, "To teach that a people's mission in God's providence is finished, that they have been relegated to the limbo of history, has murderous implications which murderers in time will spell out."[15]

These implications of Christian theology can be curbed if locatedness provides a check for unbridled universality. Christians should remember that their faith is intimately bound up with the birth, life, death, and resurrection of Jesus, with all the locatedness this one man's profoundly human experience entails. When Christians explore the locatedness of their faith, they are compelled to reconsider "the bonds of the land."

Approaching the Land

Western Christian interest in the land of Israel/Palestine takes many different forms, not all of them helpful for seeking justice in the land today. Some Christians are limited to sentimental concern for the land where their Savior lived. Others are interested in the land itself and the many stories it can tell through archaeological excavation. Still other Christians expect the land to serve as a stage for the unfolding of God's apocalyptic design. Unfortunately, Christians who approach the land only in these ways risk ignoring the real concerns of religious communities in the land, thus missing the religious and political tragedy that is contemporary Israel/Palestine.

While the land of Israel/Palestine is indeed beautiful and evocative, with many stories to tell, the region is more than a repository for history, more than an object to be manipulated by outside forces. Nevertheless, the Christians of Israel/Palestine hold age-old memories of interaction with *other* Christians: brothers and sisters in faith but still *outsiders* who have designs on the land. Tracing their heritage directly to Jesus and his apostles—each of them Palestinians—these Christians have been happy to provide hospitality for their pilgrim guests. At other times, they have experienced the underside of Christian interests in the land which have been more focused on military conquest and political power than religious commitment.

This mixed heritage of concern for the land begs the question: Is "Jerusalem" (or, more broadly, the whole of Israel/Palestine) a Christian cause?

An Early Apathy

Commentators often remark that North American Christians demonstrate little concern for the city of Jerusalem or the plight of Palestinian Christians.[16] In September 2000, for instance, Ariel Sharon's incendiary visit to a site sacred to both Muslims and Jews (Noble Sanctuary to the former, Temple Mount to the latter) brought howls of protest from around the Islamic world. By contrast, notes Colin Chapman, no such hue and cry was raised by influential voices of North American Christianity when Bethlehem fell under siege in April and May of 2002. As the Church of the Nativity gave sanctuary to Palestinian fighters, a statue of Mary, the mother of Jesus, was riddled with bullets by Israel Defense Forces fighters using it for target practice. "Why," Chapman asks, "do Christians not raise their voices to challenge what is happening to their holy places?"[17]

This apparent lack of concern may have roots in the New Testament itself. In those texts, the geographic centers of Jewish concern—including Jerusalem and the Temple—are drained of their theological import. In their stead, all significance and meaning is invested in the person of Jesus. While Christian tradition has come to place great significance in certain towns and villages associated with Jesus, this is somewhat foreign to the New Testament. Though locales figure prominently in the

As the Church of the Nativity gave sanctuary to Palestinian fighters, a statue of Mary, the mother of Jesus, was riddled with bullets by Israel Defense Forces fighters using it for target practice.

accounts of his life and crucifixion, the subject of Jesus eclipses even Jerusalem and the Temple. The destruction of the latter in 70 CE, the Gospels tell us, he foretold.[18]

The early Christian community had little regard for Jerusalem. Eusebius of Caesarea, presiding bishop of Palestine until 339, referred to the city by its Roman name, Aelia. This changed with Constantine, who sought to reestablish the city as a center of Christian concern. Encouraged by his mother, Helena, the emperor ordered basilicas built over the places of Jesus' birth and death, thus laying the foundations for the present-day Church of the Nativity and the Church of the Holy Sepulcher. As Chapman notes, however, "one of the consequences of Constantine's policy was the Jews would not be allowed to enter Jerusalem for many centuries."[19] Cyril, who succeeded Eusebius as bishop of Palestine, was the first Christian thinker to ponder Jesus' relationship with Jerusalem and establish it as a "holy city."

Christian Empire

Christians ruled the land of Israel/Palestine for many centuries following the era of Constantine. Christendom, however, lost the land to Islamic hands in 638 CE.

At the time, Islam was a relatively new religious movement; its prophet, Muhammad, had died only six years earlier. From the seventh to the eleventh centuries, three massed pilgrimages had journeyed from western Europe to Jerusalem.

In 1095, Pope Clement II urged the knights and peasants of Europe to embark on what in essence would be an armed pilgrimage, what would come to be called the First Crusade. Intending to assist the Byzantine army in defeating the Turks and to liberate the holy city of Jerusalem, the crusade was quite openly a holy war against Islam. In July 1099, the Crusaders finally managed to breach the walls of Jerusalem. A terrible massacre of almost all the city's inhabitants ensued; "Muslims and Jews were cleared out of the Holy City like vermin."[20]

The schism of 1054 between Roman and Orthodox Christians ensured that Palestinian Christians fared little better under

Western swords. By 1110, the Crusaders had conquered a wide swath of territory, rekindling among Muslims the dormant practice of *jihād*. Israel/Palestine and the prized city of Jerusalem returned to Muslim hands in 1187, under the leadership of Saladin. After Saladin returned the region to Muslim hands, the Christians of Israel/Palestine lived under Islamic rule. Still, Christians were not essentially hostile to the Muslim majority, at least not in any way approaching virulent anti-Islamic attitudes prevalent in the West. In fact, Christians were instrumental in the Arab Renaissance of the nineteenth century and have been in the forefront of Palestinian nationalist movements. Over time, the status of relations between Muslims and Christians in Israel/Palestine came to be summed up in one common phrase: "We are all brothers here."[21] Nevertheless, Christians in the West are often seized with strong desires to "liberate" Palestinian Christians and their land from Muslim oppressors:

> When Allenby arrived at the Jaffa Gate on 11 December [1917], the bells of the city pealed to welcome him. Out of respect for the holiness of Jerusalem, Allenby dismounted and entered the city on foot, taking his stand on the steps of the Citadel. He assured the inhabitants of "Jerusalem the Blessed" that he would protect the holy places and preserve religious freedom of all three faiths of Abraham in the name of His Majesty's Government. He had completed the work of the Crusaders.[22]

Islam

Allenby's muted entrance into Jerusalem echoed an earlier, equally peaceful, triumphal entry. In 638 Sophronius, patriarch of Jerusalem, surrendered the city to Umar, second caliph of the Islamic community. Believing that future Muslims would convert the site into a mosque, Umar declined the Christian leader's offer for him to pray in the Church of the Holy Sepulcher. When shown the shabby hilltop where the Jewish Temples had once stood, Umar declared that it was also the site where Abraham had offered his son in sacrifice and where the Prophet Muhammad had ascended to heaven (the *mi'raj* of his famous "night journey") to be greeted by the prophets who had come before. He ordered that a place of worship be built on the site, where the Al-Aqsa Mosque now stands. The Dome of the Rock (*qubbat al-sakhra*) was added nearby in 691.

Christians and Jews often dismiss Islamic claims to any land in Israel/Palestine. While they know Islam has an affinity for certain geographic spaces, this affinity is assumed limited to two Arabian cities, Mecca and Medina, the poles of Muhammad's political activity. The fact, however, is that Islam—in its earliest prayers and in its foundational text, the Qur'an—has from its beginnings related to the land of Israel/Palestine.

The central feature of Muslim religious life is the practice of daily prayers. Before it was directed to the Ka'ba in Mecca, the direction of prayer (*qibla*) for the fledgling Muslim community was Jerusalem. Beyond this important clue to Islam's affection for Israel/Palestine, the Qur'an contains three distinct references to the land. The first recounts Moses' encouragement of the Israelites as they journey toward Canaan: "O my people! Enter the holy land [Palestine] which Allah has assigned to you" (5:21).[23] The promise of land is also recounted in a discussion of Abraham, the father of Ishmael and Isaac: "And We [Allah] rescued him [Abraham] and Lūt (Lot) to the land which We have blessed for the *'Ālamīn* [all humankind]" (21:71).

While they are aware of Jewish hopes regarding Israel/Palestine, most Muslims read the Qur'anic promises as pertaining to Muslims.[24] This transposition arises from a unique factor of Islamic theological awareness contained in traditions surrounding a third verse from the Qur'an: "Glorified . . . be He [Allah] . . . Who took his slave [Muhammad] for a journey by night from *Al-Masjid-al-Harām* (in Mecca) to *Al-Masjid-al-Aqsā* (in Jerusalem), the neighborhood whereof we have blessed, in order that We might show him of Our *Ayāt* (signs, miracles, etc.)" (17:1).

Most Muslims believe that Muhammad was transported to Jerusalem, either physically or in a mystical experience. There, he ascended into heaven to lead all the prophets and messengers—including Adam, Moses, Abraham, Lot, and Jesus—in prayer, thus being established as the "Seal of the Prophets." It was this tradition that inspired Umar to found Al-Aqsa Mosque, the third holiest site in Islam. As a contemporary Jordanian scholar states of that event, "Umar . . . recovers an older place of worship on the Temple Mount, one linked to the older prophets, one which the Prophet himself had visited on his night journey. He clears it of rubbish and re-dedicates it to the worship of Allah. What is being subtly implied is a process not of Islamisation but of re-Islamisation."[25]

Qur'an Plus 1,300 Years

In keeping with Islam's self-understanding not as a religious innovation but as a reassertion of God's original will for human beings, all the messengers and prophets of God are presumed to be prophets of Islam,[26] sent to their respective communities. Taken together, therefore, "These verses about the land, together with the role that the land has played in subsequent Islamic history, make Muslims feel that the whole land is sacred."[27]

The mention of "holy land" in the Qur'an provides a contrast with the Christian New Testament, which as noted above, drains the land of its theological significance. The Qur'an, however, is not as specific as the Hebrew Bible regarding the geographic area it considers "holy"; scholars dispute whether the "neighborhood" around al-Aqsa mentioned in 17:1 refers to the courtyard surrounding the mosque, the whole of Jerusalem, or the entirety of Israel/Palestine.

For Muslims, the enduring significance of the land was established not just in the Qur'an, but in the centuries of Islamic rule over Palestine, beginning with Umar's meeting with Sophronius in 638. When confronted with Jewish claims to Israel/Palestine, Muslims proudly point out that the land has been in Muslim hands for 1,300 of the last 2,000 years (excepting the few years of Crusader conquest). Muslims commonly regard the land as a *waqf*—a possession entrusted to its keeper for charitable purposes—and often express responsibility for the land in language similar to that used by Christians who desire to reestablish Christendom.

Given such competing imperialist aims (active to this day), it is no surprise that the Crusades mark a turning point in Islamic concern. This period afforded Muslims their first experience of Western Christianity and introduced to Muslims "a defensiveness in their devotion to [Jerusalem], which would become a more aggressively Islamic city hitherto."[28]

Religious Nationalisms, Religious Violence

Theological claims made on the land of Israel/Palestine have political consequences. While a case can be made for sharing sacred space, most religious approaches to the land assume that sharing is not an option. Most specifically, Jewish and Islamic claims are so theologically and geographically similar that they are almost mutually exclusive. These theological foundations have informed Israeli and Palestinian political perspectives, including religious nationalisms, minimizing the possibilities for coexistence.

North Americans, viewing the modern state of Israel and Palestinians longing for their own state, might prefer to see a more explicit wall between "church" and state. Sociologist Peter Berger has noted that religious commitments are increasingly important in all politics, local and global:

> There are powerful revitalizations in all . . . major religious communities. . . . Put simply, most of the world is bubbling with religious passions. And where secular political and cultural elites have been established, they find themselves on the defensive against the resurgent religious movements—for example, in Turkey, in Israel and in India—and, last but not least, in the United States![29]

An appreciation for how the secular and the sacred interact in their own societies—where the "wall of separation" is more porous than commonly assumed—might help North Americans interact more fruitfully with various societies in the Middle East, including the religious communities of Israel/Palestine. It must be kept in mind, however, that no religious perspective or nationalist ideology adequately represents all the people for whom it claims to speak.

Zionism

The balance of secular and religious concerns is immediately apparent in Zionism, the founding ideology of modern Israel. While a return to *Eretz Yisrael* has long been a component of Jewish tradition, Zionism, a secular ideology that identifies Jews not as a religious community but as an ethnic (racial) group, has been a source of great contention in the Jewish community.

In the latter half of the nineteenth century, many Jews were optimistic that their community could be integrated into European culture. Theodor Herzl, a Viennese Jew working as a journalist in Paris, checked this optimism. For Herzl, the anti-Semitism aroused by the Dreyfus Affair exposed the egalitarian banner of "Liberty, Equality, Fraternity" as a façade. Soon after his coverage of the Dreyfus Affair, Herzl produced his manifesto, *The Jewish State* (1896).

In this slim volume, Herzl laid out the practical steps for establishing a Jewish homeland, including a strategy for promoting the concept among anti-Semites. In August 1897, Herzl called the First Zionist Conference, attended by 250 delegates from twenty-four nations, in Basel, Switzerland. Zionist Conferences continued to be held every year until the founding of the state of Israel in 1948.

Zionism gained support in small circles in Western Europe and was very influential in Eastern Europe and Russia. From its beginnings, however, the movement was shot through with ideological tendencies and factions with conflicting visions and goals. One form of resistance originated with Asher Ginsburg, also known as *Ahad Ha'am* (One of the People). He advocated a "cultural Zionism" centered on education and the revival of Hebrew, a vision that de-emphasized Herzl's focus on colonization to achieve a numerical majority.

Chaim Weizmann, who led the World Zionist Organization after Herzl's death in 1904, oversaw various strains of the movement, which ranged from socialist Zionism (engine of the kibbutz movement) to the militarist Revisionist movement of Vladimir (Ze'ev) Jabotinsky. Political Zionists worked for an eventual state to be populated by Jews fleeing pogroms and widespread anti-Semitism; cultural Zionists emphasized the creation of a "spiritual" homeland that would enrich Jewish life in the Diaspora.

The events of 1948 and 1967 changed Israeli political life and its fundamental ideology in distinct ways. With the founding of a Jewish state, the primary goal of political Zionism had been achieved. And with the transformation of associations like the Jewish Agency and Jewish paramilitary groups into official organs of political authority, the pioneering character of Zionism shifted to establishing various bureaucratic institutions. The revolutionary and uncharted nature of the prestate period was replaced by a quest for normalization. The conquest of land in the 1967 war also changed the ideological landscape of Zionism. Israel's victory catalyzed a "Greater Israel" movement convinced that the expansion of the state's borders was theologically inevitable.

Zionism continues to be a highly contested phenomenon. With Israel's late-2005 removal from the Gaza Strip of its civilian population and their military protection force, the territorial nature of the ideology was again on display. For that sliver of land at least, the pragmatic concerns of political Zionism won out over the uncompromising nature of messianic Zionism of the settler movement (discussed below).[30]

Both the consolidation of Israeli power on the territory occupied by the state and the inevitably resulting Palestinian dispossession were anticipated before and during the founding of the Jewish state. As Nur Masalha has demonstrated, "Zionist parties of all shades of opinion . . . were in basic agreement about the need and desirability of utilizing the 1948 War to establish an enlarged Jewish state with as small an Arab population as possible."[31] David Ben-Gurion wrote forcibly in 1937 on the possibility of transferring Palestinians out of Palestine for Jewish benefit:

> We have to stick to this conclusion in the same way we grabbed the Balfour Declaration, more than that, in the same way we grabbed Zionism itself. We have to insist upon this conclusion [and push it] with our full determination, power and conviction. . . . We must uproot from our hearts the assumption that the thing is not possible. It can be done.[32]

Palestinian Nationalism(s)

There is a relative consensus among world Jewry that the Jewish national project is a legitimate fact. Defending Israel—though the nature of that defense is at times in dispute between Left and Right, religious and secular—is no longer a question. The Palestinian situation is far more fragmented. As with most forms of modern Arab nationalism, Palestinian nationalism struggles between the poles of secular and religious commitment. Fateh, founded in 1958 and now closely associated with the Palestinian National Authority and the late Yasser Arafat, is an explicitly secular organization that includes Palestinian Christian voices at its highest levels. On the other hand, Hamas, founded in 1987 by, among others, Sheikh Ahmed Yassin and 'Abd al-'Aziz Rantisi (both assassinated by Israel in early 2004), presents an explicitly Islamist alternative for Palestinian nationalism.[33]

Developing within the same historical period as Zionism, Islamic thinkers like Sayyid Ahmed Khan, Jamal al-Din al-Afghani, and Egyptian Muhammad Abduh provided the foundations for various approaches to the modern, Western world. In 1928, an Egyptian educator named Hasan al-Banna formed a Sunni cultural association, the Muslim Brotherhood. Eventually seeking to establish an Islamic state in Egypt, the theopolitical perspective of the Brotherhood resonated deeply with various segments of the Islamic world. Israel's founding in 1948 proved to be formative for the Brotherhood. While engaged in some direct resistance, Muslim Brotherhood leaders distanced themselves from guerrilla activity and instead focused on the cultural formation of the next generation.

Meanwhile, more explicitly nationalist movements gained popularity. In the late 1980s, a synthesis between the previously separate commitments of social change and armed struggle was proposed. The nascent stages of the First Intifada "presented the right moment to translate their new conviction into practice and to assign top priority to the confrontation with the Israeli occupation."[34]

The undeniable success of Zionism has prompted surprising responses from Palestinian groups. Fateh has sought a secular, political solution to the conflict by attempting to engage Israel as a dialogue partner. Hamas continues to develop its Islamist ambitions for the land. For example, while most Muslims would accept that Al-Aqsa Mosque and its "neighborhood" form a *waqf*, Hamas has significantly expanded this claim by stating, "The nationalism of the Islamic Resistance Movement is part of its religion."[35]

The religious nationalism articulated by Hamas has no precedent in Islam and begs for an explanation. German researcher Andrea Nüsse, trying to understand the roots of this ideology, has come to the surprising conclusion that "Since its inception, the Arab Palestinian national movement has been emulating the Zionist movement."[36] But this complex, almost symbiotic relationship need not imply that Palestinian nationalism is merely a response to Zionism. Israeli historian Ilan Pappe has concluded, for instance, that "a local national identity had been in the making" in Palestine "before the appearance of the Zionist movement."[37]

The Theopolitical Use of Violence

The religious communities formed by Judaism, Christianity, and Islam each have distinct claims to the land of Israel/Palestine, claims with both practical and mythological dimensions, the latter often framed in terms of religious certainty. Throughout the twentieth century, violence has been the primary fruit sown and reaped in the land. The promised land, the land flowing with milk and honey, has become an abode of atrocity. For North American Christians to stand in solidarity with both Jews (Israeli and not) and Palestinians (Muslim and Christian) who strive for peace, the matter of religious violence must be addressed.

In the North American context, blame for the lack of Israeli and Palestinian coexistence has usually been laid at Palestinian feet. Former CIA analyst Kathleen Christison has argued that U.S. foreign policy in Israel/Palestine is founded on a presumption of Palestinian immorality.[38] This presumption is derived from what one Palestinian intellectual described as an "entrenched cultural attitude toward Palestinians deriving from age-old Western prejudices about Islam, the Arabs, and the Orient."[39] The mutual tradition of theopolitical tension between the Muslim and Christian worlds is partly informed by the history discussed in this chapter.

Regarding Israel/Palestine, the contemporary effect of this history is that Palestinian resistance to Israel is easily dismissed as Islamic, terroristic, and irrational. This triad of judgment is especially true for organizations like Hamas. Although until 1994 Hamas committed itself to not attacking civilians,[40] its use of suicide bombers has horrified most observers, Israeli and Palestinian alike.

Suicide attacks operate from their own logic: a guerrilla strategy informed by theopolitical commitments. Abu Mazen (Mahmoud Abbas), who in 2003 served briefly as the Palestinian prime minister and in 2005 was elected president of the Palestinian Authority, urged in 1983 that resistance "should target population centers to inflict the greatest magnitude of losses on the enemy by striking its most precious possession. This would

erase what little sense of security remains from the hearts of settlers and plant doubts in their psyches about their future."[41]

Religious violence is not limited to Palestinians. "Here in
Israel, we don't like to say this very loudly, but the radical right
Jewish groups have a lot in common with Hamas," says Carmi
Gillon, head of the Shin Bet department that uncovered the
Jewish Underground and chief of that agency when Prime Min-
ister Rabin was assassinated in 1995.[42]

The Jewish Underground drew its numbers from Gush Emunim ("Bloc of Faithful"), a group formed to promote the settlement of Arab land occupied by Israel in the 1967 war. Inspired
by the teachings of Rabbi Zvi Yehuda Kook, son of the first Ash-
kenazi rabbi of Palestine under the British Mandate, the Gush is
dedicated to creating "facts on the ground" that provide ground
for a Jewish claim on all of "Greater Israel." The relationship
between this religious group and the secular state has been reciprocal. While both rabbis saw in (secular) Zionism a sign of incipi-
ent messianic redemption, the settlements they established were
crucial for continued Israeli policy. As former Israeli Defense
Minister Moshe Dayan once stated, "Without them the IDF
would be a foreign army ruling a foreign population."[43]

Long involved in vigilante violence against Palestinians,
the Jewish Underground didn't shock public consciousness
until several conspiracies were uncovered in 1984. The most
serious of these, lasting from 1978 to 1982, involved a plan to
destroy the Dome of the Rock. If the plot had succeeded, many
have speculated, the wrath of the entire Islamic world would
have been directed at the state of Israel, bringing "in the not-
too-distant future, the risk of world conflagration."[44] Though
shocking, the plot isn't far from many Jewish and Christian
right-wing hearts.

All theopolitical extremism, Muslim and Jewish, must be
carefully counteracted. As Martin Gilbert wrote of the late
prime minister's thoughts regarding settler movements like
Gush Emunim, "Rabin knew that if they were to succeed, if the
conflict were to be theologized, there never would be peace. For,

to theological conflict, there are no compromises, and therefore no solutions."[45] Just as participation in the peace process
is repeatedly derailed by organized Palestinian violence, Prime
Minister Sharon's efforts in 2005 to "disengage" from Gaza
were met with stiff religious opposition.[46]

The nationalisms spawned to address competing claims for
the land of Israel/Palestine, whether secular or religious, have
each had to deal with competing religious claims to the land.
Even if Palestine is established as a secular state, it will, like
Israel, have to coexist with its internal "bubbling religious passions." For now, though, these religious claims seem only to add
to the intractability of the problem. Can religion contribute at
all to peacemaking in this troubled region?

Peacemakers, Not Pundits

The highly charged situation in Israel/Palestine demands a
conscientious response. Israel's military occupation of Palestinian lives and land continues unabated; the separation wall
snakes its way through the Palestinian landscape. These inter-
related crises constitute not only human rights concerns but
systematic efforts by the state of Israel to engage in what some
Israeli organizations have called a land grab. These encroach-
ing moves toward consolidating "Greater Israel" are justified
by various claims, some secular and strategic, others explicitly
religious. Meanwhile, efforts among Palestinians to address the
matter through secular means have met with little but repeated
failure, failures that provide fertile ground for the proposals of
Islamist extremists.

Some may wonder why Christians in North America would
be expected to respond to this particular situation. Are we not
holding Israel to a higher standard (and thus perpetrating a form
of anti-Semitism) when we criticize that state's policies and practices while ignoring similar abuses in other parts of the world?
Indeed, there are countless cases where Christians of conscience
should be and are at the forefront of working for justice.

One important detail regarding the situation in Israel/Palestine is that North American Christians—especially those in the United States—are *directly* involved in the ongoing struggle. Our government gives vast amounts of funding to the state of Israel, propping up the military regime and facilitating the settlers' occupation of pre-1967 Palestinian land.[47] On the other hand, the U.S. government has engaged in a "peace process" that, at times, seems designed to fail.

Guidelines for Fellow Travelers

If our discussion in this chapter has proved anything, it is that diplomacy based strictly on secular, geopolitical concerns rings hollow in Israel/Palestine, a land where (for *all* its diverse inhabitants) land is much more than the dirt beneath one's feet. The hope of establishing a just and lasting peace between Israel and the Palestinians cries out, therefore, for the responsible participation of persons of faith. Speaking from my own North American Lutheran perspective, I offer some guidelines for fellow travelers as they engage this thorny theopolitical matter.

To be effective voices for peace in the land of Israel/Palestine, North American Christians must develop a theopolitical approach independent of any particular party line. Jesus calls his disciples to be peacemakers, not pundits (Matthew 5:9). Just as not all Israeli voices call for peace, not all Palestinian voices offer constructive alternatives to the present situation.

In all cases, solidarity must consist of *critical* solidarity, not just active sympathy. To stand in critical solidarity with Palestinians and Israelis who seek peace in the land they inhabit, North American Christians must first develop a hermeneutic of justice, a lens through which events and commitments are interpreted.

As Walter Brueggemann has stated, the now-common Jewish claim of "entitlement" to the land of Israel/Palestine "cannot now be permitted to go uncontested," since discussions of "biblical land traditions must insist that land possession is held, according to that tradition, only as land practices are under the discipline of neighbor practices grounded in the Torah. Any claim of land apart from that Torah tradition is deeply suspect and open to profound critique."[48]

Broad Complicity

Engaging the situation not as righteous innocents but as empowered perpetrators, we North American Christians offer our critiques with humility, knowing that they are tainted by our legacies. Our complicity in the suffering now engulfing both Israelis and Palestinians goes beyond the implications of government policy.

Though repudiating both, we inherit a tradition of theological anti-Judaism and a legacy of murderous anti-Semitism, two factors that led to the founding of Israel as a modern nation-state and the subsequent displacement of Palestinians. On the other hand, we are also aware of our inherited traditions of anti-Islamic thought and how this perspective has fed into anti-Palestinian bias. Nevertheless, we believe that we have been called to a ministry of reconciliation in Israel/Palestine (2 Corinthians 5:18), a ministry made more urgent by our long history of unconstructive contributions.

As noted earlier in this chapter, Western Christians also inherit a tradition of selfish ambition toward the land of Israel/ Palestine. Understanding that our attachment to the land (or any land) has little grounding in biblical obligation, we assert that the defense or reconstruction of Christendom is a vainglorious hope. Still, we acknowledge that this hope is a central concern of Western imperialism—cultural, economic, and military—inherited from our Constantinian heritage.

By separating ourselves from imperial designs on the land of Israel/Palestine, we are freed to be not "pro-Israeli," not "pro-Palestinian," but "pro-justice." Instead of looking only to our self-interest, we take seriously our calling to "Speak out for those who cannot speak, for the rights of all the destitute" (Proverbs 31:8).

Listening to the Living Stones

To discern who it is "who cannot speak," we trust the witness of our Christian brothers and sisters in the land of Israel/Palestine. In the land called "holy," stones bear witness to the historicality and continued vitality of our faith. Pilgrims visiting the stones of holy places have their faith renewed and inspired in sometimes unexpected ways. Today, we are invited also to listen to the "living stones," the Christians living today in the land Jesus walked. In so doing, we can follow Isaiah's exhortation to "Look to the rock from which you were hewn, and to the quarry from which you were dug" (Isaiah 51:1).

Our choice to listen to our Palestinian Christian brothers and sisters is not made to the exclusion of other voices, including those of Israeli Jews. In the North American context, however, the uncritically pro-Zionist community seems to be speaking "our" language much more effectively than are Palestinian Christians. What does it mean for the Christian community that a common language of economic success and military power speaks more eloquently than a common language of faith?

Christians in Palestine are an exceedingly diverse lot, but all speak with a unified voice when it comes to the issue of Palestinian suffering.[49] Elias Chacour, a priest in the Melkite tradition and a citizen of Israel, asks, "Why can't Jewish people understand that we Palestinians love this land and are part of it? We are not cattle or insects to be chased away, but human beings who want to stay in our beloved land. If the Jews want to be here, too, that's fine, but why can't we live together as equals?"[50] Chapter 4 offers much in detail on how to tune in the many voices we North American Christians need to hear.

Offering a Prophetic Word

We must not only listen, but also speak. In the present situation of overwhelming lobbying pressure and "zero-sum" commitments, to speak independently is to speak *prophetically*. Theologically speaking, the opposing force to political power is prophetic critique. When religious communities collude with political power, they are leached of their prophetic possibility; the cynical use of religion by political power is exposed by prophetic critique. In its rejection of any cynical manipulation of religion, the prophetic seeks to discern the greater horizons of God's will in the world, listening to those affected by political policies and, if they are persons of faith, allowing their theological reflections to expand/shape its own. It identifies and rejects religious perspectives that have no concern for justice—political, material justice—as they pursue an apocalyptic program.

To speak prophetically regarding the situation in Israel/Palestine, Christians in North America will need to listen carefully to Jewish voices critical of their own community. We will need to listen to Marc Ellis and Gila Svirsky, Yehezkel Landau and Yossi Beilin.

Listening to voices of dissent within the Jewish community is not tantamount to calling for the destruction of the Jewish state. Nor is it to judge the state of Israel by a so-called higher standard. Instead, it is to join others in being honest about the shortcomings of a political entity, when considered from a religious perspective; it is to call sin what it is, in ourselves as well as others.

And we must respond directly to the internal challenge as well. North American Christianity is awash in a quiet controversy regarding proper approaches to the land of Israel/Palestine, a controversy that must be robustly joined by Christians of conscience. This division within the North American Christian family is the subject of the next chapter.

Lest the present theopolitical structure of "zero-sum" intractability be extended into perpetuity, our energies must be focused on the establishment of a just peace for all inhabitants of Israel/Palestine, that geographic area where, perhaps more intensely than anywhere else in the world, land is more than land.

Morning Prayer of the Lutheran World Federation Council participants (September 2005) at the Israeli separation wall near Bethlehem. In foreground: LWF President Mark Hanson, who is Presiding Bishop of the Evangelical Lutheran Church in America, and Bishop Munib Younan, Evangelical Lutheran Church in Jordan and the Holy Land. © LWF/D.- M. Grötzsch

Chapter 3

Division in the Christian Family

Robert O. Smith

Evangelicals who are Christian Zionists want to see events unfold, but they aren't so concerned about justice.

Richard Mouw, President of Fuller Theological Seminary

I am a Bible scholar and theologian and from my perspective, the law of God transcends the law of the United States government and the US State Department.

Televangelist John Hagee, when asked if his gift to expand Israeli settlements in the West Bank could possibly violate American law

In late 2002, I traveled with a group of Christians to Israel and Palestine. While our trip's primary purpose was to stand in solidarity with Palestinians and Israelis who opposed the policies of the Israeli government, the journey took on the character of a listening tour as we encountered perspectives from all sides of the conflict. Moreover, our time together served as a Christian pilgrimage: visits to biblical sites in the Holy Land and treks through the landscape provided a living backdrop for the historic beginnings of our shared faith.

A central element of our itinerary was spending time in West Bank villages, assisting residents with the autumn olive harvest. Israeli settlers occupying Palestinian land had systematically disrupted this crucial component of the local Palestinian economy. We hoped our presence as private observers from North America would allay the fears of both sides as these villagers sought to harvest their largely untended groves.

It was true that groves of trees had in some cases been used as cover to attack settlements with rockets and firearms. These incidents of Palestinian violence supplied the Israelis with justification for the establishment of wide security buffers around the settlements. These buffers then provided land for the settlements' gradual expansion into the surrounding countryside. If the fields and groves lie fallow and unkempt, an even simpler case is made by settlers: that the land should be annexed by the settlement.

Our Palestinian friends' interests were thus short-term and long-term in scope. By tending to the trees, they were reasserting their claim not only to the fruit of the harvest but also to the land from which it grew.

Reading the Bible: A Matter of Life or Death

As we trudged away from those groves, we sensed—even in the soil packing beneath our feet—the mixture of land and identity so deep within these people, now trod underfoot. We returned with many experiences and many stories to tell.

As our group sat together in the airport, exhausted from our work and emotionally drained from our two-week experience, I caught a report on the terminal's cable news channel. The reporter was citing the overwhelming commercial success of the latest book in the Left Behind series of Christian novels. Having been reared in a charismatic evangelical church steeped in the theology underlying those books and knowing where the state of Israel fit into their apocalyptic program, I grumbled some disapproval.

"Oh, come on," one of our group responded. "It's just another way of reading the Bible."

"But it's *not* 'just another way,'" I insisted. "The difference is that, because of that way of reading the Bible, people are *dying*. We just saw them."

Few Friends for Palestinians

Most Palestinians we had met—Christians and Muslims—were convinced they had very few friends among North American Christians. As they saw it, the Jewish community has been thoroughly successful in convincing American Christians that the state of Israel is a fulfillment of biblical prophecy and that Palestinians are not included in this vision. And since this modern nation-state is a fulfillment of God's will in history, criticisms of the state and its policies, even when offered from a religious perspective, will have little effect.

Our group—comprising Christians visiting from North America—had been a curiosity to Palestinians in the West Bank. Now, sitting in the airport, waiting to travel the last few miles home, I realized that Christians of conscience in North America, concerned about all inhabitants of Israel/Palestine (Jews, Christians, Muslims and others), have two responsibilities:

1. Engaging the theopolitical context within Israel/Palestine
2. Confronting the North American theopolitical perspectives that perpetuate the region's death-dealing status quo

In the end, a prophetic critique of some North American perspectives cannot be avoided. When this is the case, it is our duty to "take the fight to them." While it epitomizes much of the rancor between different strains of Christianity in the North American context, the issue of Israel/Palestine cannot be reduced to mere politicking. Nevertheless, Christians of conscience must combine shrewd political observation with keen theological analysis if we hope to live up to our calling of being ministers of reconciliation (see Matthew 10:16; 2 Corinthians 5:18–19).

Where Theology Meets Foreign Policy

Throughout the Cold War era and into the present time, U.S. censure of Israeli activities has been rare. When negative responses do come from an American administration, official criticisms are sparing and muted. In early 2004, for instance, Israel's high-profile assassinations of Hamas leaders Sheikh Ahmed Yassin and 'Abd al-'Aziz Rantisi brought few critical remarks, though the missile attacks were sure to touch off yet another round of violence, further derailing U.S. efforts to establish the latest plan for peace in Israel/Palestine, the "road map" to peace introduced by the Bush administration in April 2003.[1]

In addition to the theologically charged violence between Palestinians and Israelis, the road map faced domestic difficulties as well. Conservative evangelical leaders including Gary Bauer and Pat Robertson denounced the road map as doomed to failure since (a) the Palestinians are incapable of peaceful coexistence with Israelis, and (b) the land of Greater Israel (stretching from the Mediterranean to the Jordan River) cannot be divided because it has been promised by God forever to the Jews. The latter concern was of far greater importance than the former. American evangelicals and their Jewish counterparts—American and Israeli—lobbied the administration to withdraw the plan. Although the movement has been around since the beginning of the nineteenth century, these efforts were widely reported as evidence of a coalescing theopolitical perspective known as "Christian Zionism."

In this chapter, we will briefly explore the theological perspectives and strategic interests that inform the special relationship between the United States and the state of Israel. Attention is given to Christian Zionism in relation to American Jewish perspectives, neoconservative policy makers, American evangelicals, and mainline Christian groups. Christian Zionism raises many issues for all Christians as they seek to faithfully and publicly engage the world. Since people are dying because of this way of reading the Bible, Christians of conscience are obligated to confront this destructive theopolitical phenomenon.

American Evangelicals and Israel

Since the 1948 founding of the state of Israel, its special relationship with the United States has been consistently strong. U.S. concern for supporting "Israel as the lone democracy" in the Middle East resonates to this day. Attempts to explain such unblinking U.S. support for Israel range from thinly veiled anti-Semitic conspiracy theories to more relevant considerations of Israel's strategic benefit to U.S. interests. Thus far, it is clear: Israel has been able to convince U.S. policy makers that a strong Israeli presence in the Middle East is a *Metzia* (bargain)[2] for its primary sponsor.

In North America, support for Israel has been embodied in the politically active and highly vocal Jewish community. Its concern for Israel has been effectively articulated by an array of lobbying interests, most notably the American Israel Public Affairs Committee (AIPAC). The unanimity of this Jewish voice, however, can ebb and flow. For instance, in the years prior to the Al-Aqsa Intifada (initiated in fall of 2000), the state of Israel, long a unifying symbol, had became a potentially divisive issue that threatened to fragment the American Jewish community.[3]

This was not the first time Jewish dissent had given the lie to assumptions of Jewish unanimity regarding Israel. Political strategies aimed at ensuring public support for mutually beneficial relations between the United States and Israel were needed. Nimrod Novik, who served as foreign policy adviser to Shimon Peres, observed in 1986 what he called the "two-dimensional link between the US and Israel: first, the cultural-ideological-moral affinity; second, Israel's potential and actual contribution to American interests."[4]

As the increasingly diffuse Jewish community rallied around its sole point of accord—Israel's "contribution to American interests"—the development of the "cultural-ideological-moral affinity" was left to American evangelical Christians. Thus, from the late 1970s, pro-Israel Jewish groups joined political forces with groups like Jerry Falwell's Moral Majority.

The strong alliance between rightist Jewish groups and American evangelicals continues. In October 2004, at an evangelical gathering in Jerusalem during the Jewish festival of Tabernacles (Sukkoth), Pat Robertson made his theopolitical perspective clear. "The President has backed away from it," Robertson said of George W. Bush's faltering road map to peace. "If he [Bush] were to touch Jerusalem, he'd lose all evangelical support," Robertson continued. He even entertained the possibility that evangelicals "would form a third party."

Not all of the land occupied by Israel is of equal importance. In reference to the coming Israeli disengagement from the Gaza Strip, Robertson opined that though people "don't know about" Gaza, Jerusalem is an entirely different matter. This is because Robertson sees any plan to divide Jerusalem between Israel and any Palestinian government as "Satan's plan to prevent the return of Jesus Christ the Lord."[5]

A Christian Fascination

As Donald Wagner has observed, "Christian fascination with 'Israel' and its prophetic role at the end of history has been an important but consistently minor theme in Christianity since the days of Jesus and the early Church."[6] Questions regarding the nature and status of this "Israel" have found their way into various approaches to eschatological and apocalyptic theology.

Christian Zionists—Christians for whom the modern state of Israel plays a decisive role in Christian hope—most often believe in a theological scheme known as "dispensational premillennialism." Encouraged by the work of John Nelson Darby and C. I. Scofield, dispensationalists assert that history is divided into distinct eras (dispensations) characterized by how God

deals with distinct human groups. When "the times of the Gentiles are fulfilled" (Luke 21:24), Jesus, the Christ, will return to
rescue the true church from history—the "rapture" of so much
popular Christianity—while leaving others behind to face a time
of tribulation.

With Israel's declaration of statehood in 1948, many evangelicals anticipated that Jesus would soon return. Still, there
were problems. Many were concerned that the young state had
not claimed the whole of biblical Israel. Thus, the Six Day War
of 1967 was seen as a turning point for evangelical Christian
confidence in Israel; with its conquest of "Judea and Samaria,"
Israel had finally claimed its birthright, including all of Jerusalem. The next month, the editor of the evangelical magazine
Christianity Today offered this reflection: "That for the first time
in more than two thousand years Jerusalem is now completely
in the hands of the Jews gives a student of the Bible a thrill and
a renewed faith in the accuracy and validity of the Bible." The
pages of *Christianity Today* marveled at Israel's military prow-
ess and assured the world that Israel's wars—defensive or offensive—were God's will.[7]

Dispensationalism has proven its theopolitical endurance in
the North American context. Survey results published in 1987
showed that 57 percent of American Protestants and 35 percent
of American Catholics accepted "a prophetic interpretation of
the events of 1948," namely, the founding of the state of Israel.[8]
These theological opinions have had political results. In a mid-
2003 survey of religion and American public life, 41 percent of
Americans were more sympathetic to Israel than to the Palestinians, while 13 percent sympathized with Palestinians. Among
white evangelicals, these numbers shifted to 55 percent and 6
percent, respectively. An early 2004 survey found that Americans
generally were divided over whether U.S. policy should explicitly
favor Israel over the Palestinians: 35 percent agreed that it should,
while 38 percent disagreed. Significantly, 27 percent had no opinion on the matter. Again, these figures become more polarized
among white evangelicals. Among that group, 52 percent agreed

that U.S. policy should explicitly favor the state of Israel, while 25 percent disagreed. The remainder expressed no opinion.[9]

These survey results demonstrate that the American tradition of interpreting political events through a theological lens is alive and well. Beginning with the Puritans and widely popularized in the contemporary era through multiple printings of Hal Lindsey's *The Late Great Planet Earth*, the tradition lives on in the Left Behind books penned by Tim LaHaye and Jerry Jenkins and in television shows aired by, among others, the Trinity Broadcasting Network.

The popular dissemination of dispensationalism has helped change the shape of American religiosity. When they walk into their worship space, for instance, the four thousand congregants in Faith Bible Chapel of Arvada, Colorado, are greeted by an Israeli flag flying side by side with a Christian one. Cheryl Morrison, the church's Israel Outreach Director, works in an office decorated with "framed posters of Israeli military tanks, Apache attack helicopters and Israeli Defense Forces."

In the same state, Israeli tourism officials, hoping to shore up their flagging industry, at one time tapped a Colorado Springs–based marketing firm to attract tourists to the intifada-ridden country. The marketing solution was to create "spiritual 'swat' teams" of Christian Zionists to experience a peaceful Israel free of conflict. "These are people who are already wired to love and protect Israel," said Butch Maltby, the firm's director. "This is classic grass-roots marketing. . . . If the model works here, we plan to implement it in all cities with populations over five hundred thousand."[10] These religious expressions of political solidarity are a far cry from the alternatives discussed in chapter 4 of this book.

Evangelicals Go Mainstream

North American Christian support for the state of Israel is closely tied to what Paul Merkley has labeled "patriotic conservatism." Merkley, whose work we will discuss shortly, describes the importance of this perspective: "It is a fact of great significance that the television evangelists are, at the same time, strong on patriotic national assertion, suspicious of internationalism and especially of UN-sponsored efforts, and faithful towards Israel."[11] It is through this ethos of "patriotic conservatism" that the world of television preachers and colloquial Christianity enters even the hallowed halls of Congress.

A matter of public display since the 1980s, the theopolitical perspective of Christian Zionism took root in contemporary American culture during a period of declining mainline Christian political influence. After roughly twenty-five years of evangelical reassertion in the American political landscape, its most conspicuous contribution to American public life (at least in the amount of money appropriated to the cause) has been unwavering support for the state of Israel.[12]

With the American experience of September 11, 2001, Israel was afforded an opportunity to reassert its strategic importance to U.S. interests, quite independent of the "cultural-ideological-moral affinity" established between the two states. The simplistic, Manichean (good versus evil) worldview that provided a theopolitical framework for the Cold War has been revivified by Israel's supporters as they assert the state's importance for U.S. interests. In a post–Cold War, post-9/11 world, Israel has recast itself as an expert combatant of Islamist terrorism, and practitioners of patriotic conservatism have been provided a new threat against which to preach.

The War on Terror undertaken by President George W. Bush reflected a distinctly post-9/11 national ethos. The adoption of ideologically neoconservative national security perspectives opened the door for theopolitical concerns to shape both policy-making initiatives and politics-making speeches. Moreover, with the new National Security Strategy doctrine released one year after 9/11, the United States articulated a policy of preemptive strike, thus adopting an Israeli policy previous U.S. administrations had criticized.[13]

The Evangelical/Neoconservative Blend

The new U.S. foreign policy that arose after 9/11 did not originate with President Bush. Instead, it arose from the staff with which he had surrounded himself and was quickly identified with neoconservative thinkers in the Bush administration. Irving Kristol, responding to almost conspiratorial accusations surrounding the school of thought he helped develop, outlined a series of theses regarding neoconservative attitudes toward U.S. foreign policy, the most important being "the ability [of statesmen] to distinguish friends from enemies" and the conviction that "national interest" includes "ideological interests in addition to more material concerns."

Kristol argued that as "it was in our national interest to come to the defense of France and Britain in World War II . . . we feel it necessary to defend Israel today, when its survival is threatened. No complicated geopolitical calculations . . . are necessary." When combined with a lament for the "steady decline in our democratic culture," an alliance between neoconservatives and "religious traditionalists," especially on the issue of Israel, was ready-made.[14]

The partnership of neoconservatives and evangelicals in the post-9/11 climate was most evident in congressional politicking regarding U.S. support for Israel. A December 2001 speech on the Senate floor by Sen. James Inhofe (R.-Okla.), a member of the Senate Armed Services Committee, is surprising in its theopolitical candor. As part of his explanation of the 9/11 attacks, Inhofe stated, "We are Israel's best friend in the world because of the character we have as a nation. We came under attack [because] we are Israel's best friend."

Inhofe then went on to discuss seven points he considers "indisputable and incontrovertible evidence . . . to Israel's right to the land. You have heard this before, but it has never been in the RECORD." In a commentary on Genesis 13, from the Senate floor, Inhofe concludes with this observation: "God appeared to Abram and said, 'I am giving you *this* land,' the *West Bank*. This is not a political battle at all. It is a contest over whether or not the word of God is true."[15]

In a July 2003 speech at Israel's Knesset building, then House Majority Leader Tom DeLay (R.-Tex.) echoed many elements of Inhofe's Senate speech. DeLay's talk made headlines worldwide, mostly for his self-identification at the end of his opening comments: "Even now, I am filled with a gratitude and humility I cannot express; I stand before you today, in solidarity, as an Israeli of the heart." Continuing, he framed the context of his speech as "a great global conflict against evil" and characterized Israel as an "endangered democracy" threatened by "terrifying predators." Drawing from biblical imagery, DeLay assured the nation-state, "We hear your voice cry out in the desert, and we will never leave your side." Stating "Freedom and terrorism will struggle—good and evil—until the battle is resolved," DeLay proclaimed that Israel's liberation from Palestinian terror is an essential component of that victory.[16]

These expressions of theopolitical faith from Jim Inhofe and Tom DeLay illustrate how both Christian Zionist and neoconservative perspectives—and sometimes intriguing blends of the two—have become fixtures of the American political landscape.

The speeches demonstrate as well Kathleen Christison's observation that a fundamental component of U.S. foreign policy toward Israel/Palestine is the presumption of Palestinian immorality. This presumption has long encouraged policy makers and others to approach the conflict between Israel and the Palestinians as "a zero-sum equation in which support for Israel precluded support for any aspect of the Palestinian position."[17]

Christians Approaching Zion

But U.S. Christians are not of one mind regarding desired U.S. policy toward Israel/Palestine. Although it solidified Jewish and American evangelical fervor for the state of Israel, the 1967 war (with its resulting occupation and colonization of Palestinian land with Jewish settlements) and other actions have diminished American *mainline* Christian support. Generally, while American mainline proposals are closer to those of the Middle East

Council of Churches, evangelical and Christian Zionist preferences are closer to the realities of U.S. policy in the region.

Here is a sampling of mainline statements on the Israeli-Palestinian conflict:

- At its general convention in 1997, the Episcopal Church resolved, "That the Convention urge the government of the United States to use its diplomatic and economic influence . . . to demonstrate a firm commitment to justice for Palestinians as it does for the security of the State of Israel."
- In March 2002, the U.S. Conference of Catholic Bishops stated, "It is clearer now than ever before that the present state of affairs is unacceptable. Palestinian attacks on innocent civilians cannot be tolerated—both because they are morally abhorrent and because they undermine the legitimate claims of the Palestinian people. Israeli occupation . . . cannot be sustained—militarily or morally. Nor can the indiscriminate and excessive use of force in civilian areas. . . . This deadly cycle of action and reaction, suicide bombing, and aggressive attacks must be ended."
- In May 2004, the United Methodist Church stated its opposition to the "continued military occupation of the West Bank, Gaza and East Jerusalem" and "any vision of a 'Greater Israel' that includes the occupied territories and the whole of Jerusalem and its surroundings." Furthermore, the assembly urged "the U.S. government to end all military aid to the region" so that it might redistribute the money to nongovernmental organizations.
- At its General Synod meeting in June 2004, the Reformed Church in America, in addition to declaring Christian Zionism to be a distortion of the biblical message, began a discussion that is the first of its kind among mainline American denominations: an exploration of how the Belhar Confession, a statement of Christian doctrine born out of the struggle against apartheid in South Africa, might apply to the partitioning of Israel/Palestine.

- In August 2005 the Evangelical Lutheran Church in America adopted a campaign titled "Peace Not Walls: Stand for Justice in the Holy Land." It urges members, congregations, synods, the churchwide organization, and related agencies and institutions to take part by:

  ○ "praying for peace with justice between Israel and Palestine and for the continuing witness of the Christian Church—including the Evangelical Lutheran Church in Jordan and the Holy Land—in the region;

  ○ "building relationships with the Evangelical Lutheran Church in Jordan and the Holy land, the ministries of the Lutheran World Federation, and other ecumenical and inter-faith companions engaged in the pursuit of peace in the Holy Land;

  ○ "continuing to build bridges to other Christian brothers and sisters throughout the Middle East, including Lebanon, Jordan, Palestine, and Egypt, and advocating for human rights when those rights are threatened;

  ○ "learning about the situation in the Holy Land, sharing information, and building networks;

  ○ "intensifying advocacy for a just peace in the region, building upon Evangelical Lutheran Church in America and predecessor body policies, and engaging with the public media in this effort;

  ○ "stewarding financial resources—both U.S. tax dollars and private funds—in ways that support the quest for a just peace in the Holy Land; and

  ○ "giving generously to help ensure the continuation of the school and other ministries of the Evangelical Lutheran Church in Jordan and the Holy Land and the humanitarian work of the Lutheran World Federation through Augusta Victoria Hospital and other ministries."

Christian Zionists and Israeli Jews: Bedding Down

Through high-profile leaders like Jack Van Impe and Pat Robertson, along with a variety of organizations such as Bridges for Peace,
the Unity Coalition for Israel, and the International Christian
Embassy in Jerusalem, evangelicals have been highly successful in
marshaling U.S. support for the state of Israel. Still, many Jews are
wary of wedding their interests to the evangelical juggernaut.

Controversy has surfaced among some Jews regarding what
they consider the center of the evangelical agenda: *evangelism*.
In 2004, two former chief rabbis of Israel, Avraham Shapira and
Mordechai Eliahu, agreed on a religious ruling that Jews should
not accept money from groups engaged in "missionary activity."
The primary target of their criticism was the International Fellowship of Christians and Jews, though the ruling served to put
all evangelical groups on notice.[18]

More disturbing for many Jews are the radical political
positions engendered by evangelical Christian theological perspectives. "There's support for some of the most extreme political positions in Israeli society," said Rabbi David Rosen of the
American Jewish Committee. "That I find far more disturbing
than any suggestion that there could be missionary activity." As
Robert Freedman has noted, these political alliances may have
far-reaching effects: "Once you get in bed with them you are,
to a certain extent, subscribing to their view of what America
ought to be. And that, in my view, is not in the best interests of
the Jewish people."[19]

In the end, however, this marriage of convenience is too
lucrative to pass up. As former AIPAC researcher Lenny Davis
once stated: "Sure, these guys give me the heebie-jeebies. But
until I see Jesus coming over the hill, I'm in favor of all the
friends Israel can get."[20]

Christian Zionists versus the Mainline

Christian Zionist writers have not been shy about confronting mainline Christian reluctance to endorse U.S. foreign
policy bias toward Israel. Most of these challenges are simplistic and polemical. A more substantive discussion can be

had with Paul Charles Merkley, a self-identified Christian Zionist and Canadian historian who is also a member of the Evangelical Lutheran Church in Canada. One of his books, *Christian Attitudes towards the State of Israel*, seeks to defuse stereotypes surrounding evangelical Christian support of Israel and criticizes mainline Christians for their abandonment of the Zionist cause.

Beyond differing approaches to biblical texts, disagreements between politically liberal and conservative approaches to Israel can be seen as manifestations of a clash of historical narratives. While, for instance, "Liberal historians and ecumenical churchmen tell the story of Israel's expanding sphere of action in the same language that is used for the wars of Napoleon or Nebuchadnezzar," Merkley notes, "Christian Zionists prefer the vocabulary of self-defence and national security that the Israeli government itself employs."[21]

Merkley attributes liberal Christian sympathy for pro-Palestinian perspectives to political gullibility. The "liberal-ecumenical attitude," he asserts, is "not grounded in a transcendent theology" and thus "shifted when the political scenery shifted." Merkley sees liberal attention to the plight of Palestinians as a product of "1960s . . . disdain for 'the establishment'" and a "disposition to patronize" that leads to alignment with "the generalized cause of the 'oppressed' everywhere."[22] The lack of theological foundations among liberal North American Christians has led to the development of relationships with Middle Eastern Christians like Naim Ateek, Elias Chacour, and Munib Younan, violating the sharp distinction Merkley wishes to draw between the "Churches of the East" and "Churches of the West."

Merkley rejects out of hand any effort at Palestinian contextual theology (liberation theology). Because Palestinian claims are openly political, Merkley (and many others) doubt their theological veracity. But Merkley goes even further, labeling as heretics Palestinian Christians who question the claims of Zionism (Jewish or Christian). Thus, when Palestinian Christian pastors observe in all honesty that the Hebrew Scriptures have "become almost repugnant to Palestinian Christians" since they have been used "largely as a Zionist text"—thus tragically alienating their people from the bulk of their scriptural canon—Merkley labels them heretics, accusing them of "openly embracing the doctrine of Marcion."[23] He closes the book with this comment: "It is simply too soon to know whether the work done by forces dedicated to Jewish-Christian reconciliation . . . will stand against the flanking effort of the neo-Marcionists, whose heart is in the different work of accomodating [sic] the secular liberals, the Churches of the East, and the Muslims."[24]

Though he has taken time to consider Palestinian and pro-Palestinian Christian perspectives, Merkley does not allow for the possibility that Christians who disagree with him can do so from legitimate grounds, theological or political. His dismissal of liberation theology demonstrates a lack of regard for the ability of Christianity (or, for that matter, Judaism or Islam) to provide a prophetic critique to politics or culture. His conservative theology seeks to protect the status quo of both theology and politics, even when this results in tragedy and atrocity. Christians of conscience called to reconciliation rather than imperial domination must conclude, on the basis of their cruciform faith, that it is simply not viable to reject the possibility of a livable, just peace for all peoples in the Holy Land.

The Intra-Evangelical Intifada

That Christian Zionists and their pro-Zionist evangelical constituency are not dedicated to establishing an equitable resolution to the Israeli-Palestinian conflict has become a liability. While predictably drawing condemnation from Palestinian Christians and their mainline sympathizers,[25] criticism is flowing also from evangelical wells. As Richard Mouw has stated, "Evangelicals who are Christian Zionists want to see events unfold, but they aren't so concerned about justice."[26]

Merkley—while accusing liberal Christians of theopolitical gullibility and Palestinian Christians of heresy—places the restoration of Jews to the land of Israel/Palestine upon a firmer ground than mere justice: "namely, that it was predicted and ordained by Scripture. To have resisted it would have been sin, and in any case would be futile."[27]

John Hagee demonstrated this theopolitical rationale in February 1998. When asked if he was uncomfortable that the $1 million gift his congregation was making to Israel's effort of resettling Russian Jews in the West Bank could possibly transgress American policy, he replied, "I am a Bible scholar and theologian and from my perspective, the law of God transcends the law of the United States government and the US State Department." Subsequent gifts have been even larger.[28]

Over recent decades, it has come to be assumed that American evangelicals automatically, uncritically, and monolithically accept the Christian Zionist version of America's "cultural-ideological-moral affinity"[29] with Israel. The reckless theopolitical reasoning engendered by this affinity has led many American evangelicals to distance themselves from Christian Zionist perspectives. These Christians thus challenge the calculated exploitation of their community by Likud politicians and those who have become their friends.

Just as American Jewish unanimity regarding Israeli policies had waned prior to the Second Intifada (literally, "shaking off"), the evangelical community (represented by scholars like Don Wagner, Colin Chapman, and Gary Burge—and even in the pages of *Christianity Today*) seems now to realize the implications of being associated with an ideological theology that, in the name of God, despises efforts at peacemaking; this longtime association must itself be "shaken off."

Moving Forward

Despite these positive developments of Christian conscience within the American evangelical community, access to the first-term Bush administration was still granted only to its most stridently Christian Zionist representatives. This access reached a climax on July 14, 2003, with a meeting called by the White House Office of Public Liaison "at the request of a close friend of [Ariel] Sharon, Rabbi Yechiel Eckstein of Chicago," founder and president of the International Fellowship of Christians and Jews. The gathering, attended by about forty evangelical leaders, featured a briefing by national security adviser Condoleezza Rice.[30] Leaders of U.S. mainline Protestant and Catholic groups, while frequently seeking an opportunity to meet with President Bush during the years 2001–5, were never granted such a meeting.

If the perception of evangelical unanimity regarding Israel/ Palestine begins to erode, the United States may be freed to aggressively pursue the possibilities of an equitable and just peace. With this in mind, it should be noted in the survey results discussed in this chapter that, although there is no widespread sympathy for the Palestinian cause, Americans do not support unbalanced U.S. policies favoring the state of Israel. Even among white evangelicals, Israel's most vociferous domestic supporters, 25 percent agreed that U.S. policy should not be so lopsided, and 23 percent had formed no opinion on the matter. Perspectives, though they might seem set in stone, are still open to influence.

In the meantime, however, the Palestinian catastrophe experienced in 1948 (*al-Nakba*) and further consolidated in 1967 is nearing completion. The extent of Palestinian defeat is exemplified in the public shift from the possibility of negotiated, peaceable coexistence to the unilateral enforcement of Israel's proclivities and prerogatives for the Palestinian population.[31]

We North American Christians must hold ourselves accountable to the fact that this shift—in policy and ethos—has been undergirded not only by strategic arguments but also by Christian *theology*. Because we are complicit in this new era of Palestinian oppression, we must actively confront the theopolitical ideology of Christian Zionism and its unwitting constituents. Since Christian Zionism understands itself as faithful to Scripture in its application of premillennial dispensationalism, Barbara Rossing's book, *The Rapture Exposed*, is a very important contribution to the discussion.[32]

Christians of conscience cannot assume that biblical or theological critiques of Christian Zionism will be widely persuasive. Given its cultural reinforcement, nothing short of a comprehensive approach laying out a viable and faithful alternative will accomplish the marginalization of Christian Zionism it richly deserves. Every tool of critical analysis—cultural, rhetorical, political, historical, postcolonial—must be employed if the tide is to be turned.

But in the meantime, there are practical steps that can be taken by individuals and groups, even denominations. Palestinians—Muslim and Christian—were greatly encouraged when the 2004 General Assembly of the Presbyterian Church (U.S.A.) authorized "exploration of a *selective* divestment of church funds from those companies whose business in Israel is found to be directly or indirectly causing harm or suffering to innocent people, Palestinian or Israeli."[33] More than just another safe statement, the action, potentially costly (economically and politically) for this mainline denomination, was a bold step toward recognizing and correcting the matrix of injustice that has engulfed Israel/Palestine.

Other denominations and Christian organizations voiced interest in pursuing similar options. Most of these efforts were stifled in committee. But the World Council of Churches (WCC) adopted a strong call for its member churches to use economic pressures in the quest for an end to Israeli occupation of Palestinian territories.

The institutional actions of the Presbyterian Church (U.S.A.) can be compared to the personally risky and politically unpopular work of individuals who participate in the Christian Peacemaker Teams, based in the historic peace-church tradition, and the Ecumenical Accompaniment Programme, administered by the WCC. These examples serve merely as a preface to a weightier conversation about practical work, to be continued in the next chapter.

The theopolitical outlook of Christian Zionism—undergirded by "patriotic conservatism"—is fundamentally indifferent to human suffering, especially when that suffering is a direct result of its supported positions. If we are to engage in a prophetic critique of the systems of injustice (be they cultural, economic, theological) underlying the present realities of Israel/Palestine, we must not be content with mere words but must instead engage in a praxis of costly solidarity. Only then will we claim our Christian calling as ministers of reconciliation. And perhaps then this rift that has divided the Christian family may begin to mend.

Women and children from the West Bank village of Jayyous, taking part in a demonstration to protest Israel's erection of a separation barrier on land owned and cultivated by the villagers.

The authors with Pastor Mitri Raheb at Christmas Lutheran Church in Bethlehem.

Chapter 4

The Call to Action

Charles P. Lutz

We are not asking for more statements. We are asking for action. . . . Citizens of [Western] countries must care that their money be spent not to subsidize the Israeli occupation but to create a just peace. . . . Christian hope holds firm that it's never too late for faith in action and for acts of compassion. Christian hope does not surrender to the forces of death and despair but challenges them.

Mitri Raheb, pastor of Christmas Lutheran Church, Bethlehem, in *Bethlehem Besieged: Stories of Hope in Times of Trouble*

Over the past half-century-plus, no region of the world has had as much global media attention as that land called holy. The Israel/Palestine conflict has received more newsprint and airtime, for more years running, than any other single story anywhere on the planet.

Formal studies indicate the truth of such statements—for the American context in particular, but also in the West generally, and certainly in the Middle East. Yet, when asked their opinions about the Holy Land situation, U.S. citizens typically respond in words like these:

> "It's just so complicated—I don't know what to believe."
> "The media are biased; you can't trust their reporting."
> "They'll never stop fighting over there, so I've stopped paying attention."

To What Are Christians Called?

How can we know what to believe—and how to behave? What is God calling us Christians to do on the highly emotional question of the Holy Land?

This chapter is offered as a how-to manual for responding to those concerns. It unfolds in four parts. They can be called the four *P*s:

Paying attention
Praying fervently
Public-policy advocating
Pilgrimage making/offering presence

Paying Attention

How does one find accurate, balanced reporting on the Israel/Palestine situation? It takes some doing. Without initiative that actively seeks sources beyond the mainstream media, we will miss the full story. In a way, this is ironic. The foreign-press community in Jerusalem is one of the largest in the world, probably second in size only to the number in Washington, D.C. Yet readers and viewers who turn to the general media for anything like the complete story of what's happening in Israel/Palestine will be shortchanged.

For those who try to tell this story fairly, unique challenges arise, for several reasons. These include three realities of modern-day news coverage:

First, hard-news coverage anywhere in the conventional journalism world is invariably event-oriented. For the Holy Land conflict, this means the daily telling of the story almost always leads with the latest incident of deadly violence. Other aspects of the story, such as historical and political background on what causes the violence, get scant attention. A suicide bombing in Tel Aviv always finds more ink and airtime than the ongoing suffering—and dying—of Palestinian refugees. A bombing will garner far more coverage than that day's destruction by Israel of Palestinian homes or Israel's opening of new housing units for settlers on Palestinian land.

The second reason is the Israeli connection. News gathering for foreign journalists based in Jerusalem tilts toward Israel, not due to willful bias but resulting from certain givens. First, information provided to journalists originates mostly in Israeli government sources, mainly its military, the Israel Defense Forces (IDF). Getting good information from Palestinian sources, official or otherwise, is difficult, both because of inadequacies in the Palestinian Authority and because Israel's army controls the area in which most of the news is made. Curfews, movement restrictions, even fear of physical danger make news gathering in the occupied territories a tough business.

Another Israeli connection concerns the composition of the journalist pool working in the Holy Land. A study done in late 2000, after the Al-Aqsa Intifada erupted, showed that almost 70 percent of the journalists serving international media were Jewish (Israelis or internationals) or were married to Israeli Jews.[1] A final Israeli-connection problem, at least for television reporting, concerns the threat of censorship by Israel's military. CNN claims it must submit its video footage to the Israeli military prior to use or it will be "kicked out of the country."[2]

Third, and not least, this conflict in recent years gets reported mainly through two specific prisms, those of religious war and of terrorism. Both prisms pack high emotional content. For many Americans, placing the conflict in a setting of religious claims tends to reinforce Sunday-school images of the Holy Land as belonging to a Chosen People (hint: they're not the ones speaking Arabic!). And for nearly all Americans, "terrorism" in the Holy Land is now linked with the horrors of 9/11 and identified with suicide bombings by Palestinians—but almost never with the state-sponsored terror practiced by Israel's government against civilian Palestinians.[3]

Words Too Go to War

In seeking to understand Holy Land realities, one fact is unavoidable: for that conflict, even words go to war. Each side has its preferred terminology—for talking about violence and fighting tactics, certainly. But even for geographic and political entities, there are distinct vocabularies, such as the following:

Many Israelis Say	Many Palestinians Say
Terrorists	Freedom fighters
Homicide bombers	Heroic martyrs
Targeted preventions	Assassinations
Disputed territories	Occupied territories
Jewish neighborhood	Illegal settlement/colony
Separation fence	Apartheid wall[4]
Judea and Samaria	The West Bank
Temple Mount	Haram al-Sharif (Noble Sanctuary)
State of Israel	The Zionist Entity

It is obvious that the words used in discussing Holy Land realities take on deep emotional significance to people elsewhere in the world as well, not least in the United States. In the spring of 2002, the *Star Tribune*, a Minneapolis newspaper, was publicly chastised by a group called Minnesotans Against Terrorism. The group's goal was to campaign for media use of specific language. It placed opinion articles and a full-page ad in the Minneapolis paper, charging it with journalistic malpractice.

Creating Minnesotans Against Terrorism were several Jewish leaders, led by a prominent Minneapolis attorney. Beyond complaining to area media, they organized meetings to promote their cause. For one such meeting, not open to the general public, the invitation list was chiefly local Christian clergy, and the main speaker was an adviser to Israeli Prime Minister Ariel Sharon. (It's worth noting that, outside this gathering, a protest demonstration was organized by another Jewish group, Minnesota Jews for a Just Peace, who disagreed with Minnesotans Against Terrorism.)

What was the complaint of Minnesotans Against Terrorism? The *Star Tribune*'s use of "suicide bomber" instead of "terrorist" when reporting on killings of Israelis by Palestinians who turn their bodies into lethal weapons.[5]

Those who take a more pro-Palestinian stance also lobby with U.S. media outlets, of course. But clearly they've never been organized and funded as well as the pro-Israel voices.

Understanding the Spin

The truth is that all political reporting has spin (so does this book). Reporting the Palestine-Israel conflict is no exception. But in the mainline U.S. media, the spin for several decades has spun mostly in one direction, toward the official Israeli viewpoint. Indeed, it is no stretch to say that since 1967 Israel has pursued two occupations: a military occupation of the Palestinian territories, and an ideological occupation of the U.S. media.

A systematic and pervasive public relations campaign is operated by the Israeli government and its U.S. allies. How effective that PR effort has been is shown when U.S. coverage is compared with that found in other Western nations, Great Britain, for example. The Media Education Foundation has done just such a comparison. Its video *Peace, Propaganda, and the Promised Land*[6] argues that, especially after the 9/11 attacks and mainly for U.S. consumption, "Israel has repackaged an illegal military occupation as a war on terrorism." MEF's analysis identifies seven strategies in Israel's news repackaging:

1. To hide references to "occupation"—making Israel not the aggressor but the victim, the defender against Palestinian acts of violence
2. To make colonization (settlements) in occupied Palestinian territory invisible
3. To present Palestinian violence in a vacuum, with no reference to causation
4. To define who is newsworthy—in the Second Intifada (2001–5), 1,000 dead Israeli civilians are newsworthy, but 3,300 dead Palestinians are not[7]
5. To maintain the myth that the United States is neutral and evenhanded
6. To maintain the myth of a "generous offer" by Israel's then–Prime Minister Barak to Palestine's President Arafat at Camp David in 2000
7. To make particular Israeli voices (those of its peace movement) seem irrelevant

Nongovernmental Voices: Israel

Many providers of news and opinion within Israel offer more balanced approaches than does the press office of a hard-line government. These include public media in Israel, which routinely present stories and views that never find their way into the U.S. general media. A striking example is the Israeli daily *Ha'aretz*, which has an English edition (Web site: www.haaretz.com). There is significant press freedom in Israel, and Israelis routinely receive political opinion on the conflict that's far more diverse than most U.S. readers and viewers can even imagine.

Other Israeli sources deserving our attention are the many peace and human-rights groups that actively seek a just resolution of the conflict—and make information readily available online. These are noteworthy:

*   *B'tselem*—the Israeli Information Center for Human Rights in the Occupied Territories, highly respected internationally for its reliable documentation of rights violations by

Israel's government. Its publication, *Land Grab*, deals with settlement activities and barrier building inside Palestinian territory. Web site: www.btselem.org.

- *Gush Shalom (Peace Bloc)*—a leader in the Israeli peace movement. It favors Israeli withdrawal from the occupied Palestinian territory and a negotiated peace with Palestinians. It works with Palestinians in defending their human rights and promotes an international boycott of products made in Israel's illegal settlements. Gush Shalom has an English-language e-newsletter, available via info@gush-shalom.org. Web site: www.gush-shalom.org (click on "English").
- *ICAHD*—the Israeli Committee against House Demolitions, led by the U.S.-born (Minnesota native) Jeff Halper, now an Israeli citizen. It stands with Palestinians whose homes are threatened with destruction by Israel's government and helps them rebuild when destruction occurs. Web site: www.icahd.org.eng.
- *Israeli Council for Israeli-Palestinian Peace*—publishes a newsletter, *The Other Israel*, edited by Adam Keller. To order a free sample copy, e-mail name and postal address to AICIPP@igc.org. Web site: http://otherisrael.home.igc.org.
- *Joint Coalition of Women for a Just Peace*—a group of Israeli agencies representing concerned women, including Bat Shalom and the Women in Black. Web site: www.coalitionofwomen.org.
- *Rabbis for Human Rights*—led by U.S.-born Rabbi Arik Ascherman, now an Israeli citizen. Ascherman believes authentic Judaism demands just treatment of "the other, the stranger and sojourner" in the promised land. RHR routinely takes direct action with Palestinians in defending their human rights. Web site: www.rhr.israel.net.

Nongovernmental Voices: Palestine

These Palestinian nongovernmental agencies working for peace with justice are also good sources:

A home under construction, assisted by Israeli Committee against House Demolitions (ICAHD). ICAHD is headed by Jeff Halper, an American-born Jewish citizen of Israel. The act of rebuilding Palestinian homes demolished at the whim of the Israeli military is a courageous expression of resistance to inhumane policies of the Israeli occupation.

- *Applied Research Institute*—nonprofit organization dedicated to promoting sustainable development in the occupied territories. Web site: www.arij.org.

- *Bethlehem Media Center*—program of Christmas Lutheran Church's International Center and a faithful supplier of the Palestinian stories that aren't covered by the international media. Web site: www.bethlehemmedia.org.

- *International Solidarity Movement*—formed by Palestinians and internationals committed to nonviolent direct action. ISM trains persons for "buffering" work in Palestinian communities that face harassment from Israeli settlers and the Israeli military. Included are such actions as helping farmers harvest olives and protesting Israel's placement of the separation wall on Palestinian land. Web site: www.palsolidarity.org.

- *Palestinian Centre for Rapprochement between People*—peace center in Beit Sahour, adjacent to Bethlehem. Rapprochement, an ISM cosponsor, offers a weekly audio report, "Five Minutes from Palestine," available online at www.imemc.org/audio. Rapprochement also sends news summaries on a near-daily schedule. To subscribe by e-mail: rapprochement@palsolidarity.org. Web site: www.rapprochement.org.

- *Palestinian Environmental NGOs*—nonprofit group providing coordination for Palestinian environmental organizations in the occupied territories. Its chief agenda in recent years has been opposing the confiscation of Palestinian land and water by Israeli settlements and the security wall. Web site: www.pengon.org.

Christian Voices from the Holy Land

Recent writings by Palestinian Christians are essential in the learning process for Christians elsewhere in the world. Many books are available in English. (For publication data, see Resources.)

Episcopal Bishop Riah Abu el-Assal has written *Caught in Between: The Extraordinary Story of an Arab Palestinian Christian Israeli*. It contains the story of a childhood in (pre-Israel)

Nazareth, years in exile, pastoral ministry in Nazareth, and (since 1998) service in Jerusalem as bishop of the Episcopal (Anglican) communion in the Middle East.

Elias Chacour, another Palestinian citizen of Israel, continues ministering as a Melkite Catholic priest in the Galilee. One of his books—written with Mary E. Jensen, a U.S. Lutheran pastor—is *We Belong to the Land*. Another is *Blood Brothers*.

Lutheran Bishop Munib Younan has written about the promise of "trialogue"—interfaith conversation among Jews, Christians, and Muslims of Israel/Palestine. His *Witnessing for Peace in Jerusalem and the World* is a call to seek peace with justice through nonviolent means.

Mitri Raheb, pastor of Christmas Lutheran Church in Bethlehem, has written movingly about his identity as a Palestinian Christian and his experiences during Israel's 2002 military siege of Bethlehem. His two books are *I Am a Palestinian Christian* and *Bethlehem Besieged: Stories of Hope in Times of Trouble*.

Another powerful Palestinian Christian voice is that of Naim Ateek, the Anglican priest who founded Sabeel, an ecumenical center for Palestinian liberation theology. Ateek's book, *Justice and Only Justice: A Palestinian Theology of Liberation*, articulates a theology based on principles of justice, peace, and nonviolence.

Alison Jones-Nassar, an American expatriate married to a Palestinian Lutheran, has recorded her family's experiences of living in occupied Palestine. Her book, *Imm Mathilda: A Bethlehem Mother's Diary*, gives special attention to the impact of the occupation on the emotional and spiritual health of her daughters.

Ann Hafften has gathered several voices of Palestinians and expatriates working there in her *Water from the Rock: Lutheran Voices from Palestine*. They offer stories of hope seldom told by secular journalists. The book includes useful prompters for group discussion.

Additionally, a most helpful survey of Christian life in the region today is Charles Sennott's *The Body and the Blood: The Holy Land's Christians at the Turn of a New Millennium*. Sennott, the *Boston Globe*'s bureau chief in Jerusalem when he wrote the book, explores the conflict through the lenses of the tiny Christian minority, which he sees as an essential bridge between Jews and Muslims.

Other U.S. Jewish Voices

Israeli government policies and actions are supported almost automatically by U.S. mainstream Jewish agencies, in their public communicating and political lobbying. These include most notably the American Israel Public Affairs Committee (AIPAC), plus various regional groups, often working under the name Jewish Community Relations Council. Other U.S. Jewish groups are more critical of Israel's political behavior and push for Israelis and Palestinians to negotiate a just peace. These include the following:

- *Americans for Peace Now*—a U.S. affiliate of Israel's Peace Now. It brings Israeli speakers to the United States and addresses the U.S. foreign-policy agenda regarding the Middle East. Web site: www.peacenow.org.
- *Brit Tzedek v'Shalom (Alliance for Justice and Peace)*—works mainly at Jewish community "inreach." It is "guided by the obligation to pursue peace and justice that is rooted in both secular and religious Jewish traditions. We believe . . . security for Israel can only be achieved through the establishment of an economically and politically viable Palestine state. This necessitates an end to Israel's occupation of land acquired during the 1967 war and an end to Palestinian terrorism." Web site: www.btvshalom.org.
- *Jews for Justice in the Middle East*—source of publications examining Israeli and Palestinian behavior in light of international law. Examples are "The Origin of the Palestine-Israel Conflict" and "The Israeli Occupation: Background and Analyses of the Current Conflict." Publications are available online at www.cactus48.com.
- *Not in My Name*—coalition of Jewish groups that protest Israel's occupation of Palestine. It stands with Israel's peace

movement: "Israeli peace groups rightfully criticize their government and we should too, since the Israeli government claims to act in our name." Web site: www.nimn.org.

- *Tikkun Community*—national group with regional chapters. It publishes a bimonthly magazine also titled *Tikkun*, Hebrew for "to mend, repair, and transform the world." Led by Rabbi Michael Lerner, Tikkun seeks to work on an interfaith basis for a just peace in the Holy Land. Lerner is author of *The Geneva Accord and Other Strategies for Healing the Israeli-Palestinian Conflict*. Web site: www.tikkun.org.

Praying Fervently

We now arrive at the second *P*: Christian worshiping communities anywhere in the world who have concern for peace and reconciliation between Palestinians and Israelis should routinely include petitions to that end in the corporate prayers of the church.

And not only at prayer time should the Holy Land enter public worship, but throughout the liturgy, the public service of God's people. Holy Land links appear regularly, of course, in scripture lessons read at worship. And making ties with current realities can become intentional in the proclamation of God's Word, the sermon. Even the offering of material gifts, as those include support for ministries in the Holy Land, is a fitting moment for lifting up concern for peace and healing there.

"Let Us Pray for Ourselves . . ."

How do we pray? What do we ask of God? The presuppositions behind our prayers for Middle East peace are important.

Christians in the Holy Land urge sisters and brothers around the world, "Do not be pro-Israeli or pro-Palestinian. Rather, be pro-justice and pro-peace." This is a solid guideline when we do our public-policy advocating and when we make visits to the Holy Land. It surely is good counsel for our praying as well.

This word for internationals is prayed at Jerusalem's Episcopal Cathedral of Saint George's (and posted in its narthex):

Let us pray not for Arab or Jew, not for Palestinian or Israeli, but let us pray rather for ourselves, that we might not divide them in our prayers but keep them both together in our hearts. Amen.

A Prayer Vigil

A network of U.S. church agencies launched a national prayer vigil for Middle East peace in Advent 2000. Both individual Christians and congregations are encouraged to join. Gathering in local ecumenical groups is another proposed pattern. Participants are asked to pray especially on specific days, with each date of the month assigned to a U.S. state or two. Congregations typically offer their prayers on the Sunday nearest the assigned date for their state.

Sample petitions, liturgies for services of prayer, and other worship resources are available. For more details, check with Peaceful Ends through Peaceful Means (www.pepm.org). Here are samplings of prayers available there:

Blessed Jesus, lifting up the Holy Land for all humankind, breathe love into our prayers with a desire for nothing other than peace: peace in our hearts, peace for all creation, and especially peace in the land that is called holy.

God of hope, we lift up the city of Jerusalem, distracted and divided, yet still filled with promise as all the cities of the world. Jesus, ride again into our cities, temples, upper rooms, and Gethsemanes, that we may be given sight to recognize you.

God of mercy, even as we long to understand that which is often beyond our comprehension, we lay before you the hearts, minds, and bodies of all those suffering from conflict in Palestine and Israel. Shower upon all holy people of the Holy Land the spirit of justice and reconciliation. Amen.

Prayer Accompaniment

There are also requests from sisters and brothers in the Holy Land to join them in specific prayer petitions. It is a form of accompaniment every bit as important as physical presence with those who suffer injustice. A group at Bethlehem Bible College, a Christian school in Jesus' town of birth, issued this appeal late in 2004:

> The infrastructure of Bethlehem has been virtually destroyed; the rate of unemployment is 70 percent. The Wall that snakes around the town and the surrounding villages, and at certain parts inside the towns and villages, is a virtual nightmare. Land has been confiscated. Olive trees have been uprooted, reducing land on which people depended for their livelihood into a desert. The Wall chokes the towns and limits the mobility of the people. It prevents them from performing basic tasks and fulfilling basic needs, such as going to school or work or even seeking medical help. To say that the Wall merely inflicts hardship on the people is a gross understatement. There is a sense of helplessness and hopelessness that is generating a lot of anger. There is fear and uncertainty of what the future holds.

- Pray that God will lift the cloud of depression. Pray that the people in their distress will look up to Him as their only provider.
- Pray for the restoration of the economy, especially tourism on which the town almost totally depends.
- Pray that God will give ideas to business people and entrepreneurs for projects that do not rely totally on tourism. Pray that He will give them the resources and the ability to carry out these projects.
- Pray for a good season of rain and for abundance that the trees will produce enough to meet the need.
- Pray for the Wall to tumble down and to be dismantled peacefully.

> Dear friends, we will keep you informed, and will continue to share with you the needs that the Lord is leading us to pray for. We will also be glad to hear from you at: <aflefel7@yahoo.com>.
> *On behalf of the intercessors in Bethlehem*

Olive trees uprooted by Israeli workers, guarded by the Israel Defense Forces, to make way for the erection of Israel's separation barrier on Palestinian land.

Prayers for public use have come also from the National Interreligious Initiative for Peace in the Middle East. This trifaith consortium offers petitions from Jewish, Muslim, and Christian sources. Here are sample petitions:

> Sustain together in undiminished hope, O God of hope, those who continue to labor with undiminished determination to build peace in the land from which, of old, out of brokenness, violence and destruction, nevertheless hope emerged for so many of faith. Bless all the spiritual seed of Abraham together with the light of your Presence. For in the light of your Presence we have found a way of justice and mercy and a vision of Peace. We praise you, O God, Giver of Peace, who commands us to Peace. Amen. (From Rabbi Herbert Bronstein, Glencoe, Illinois.)

> Almighty God! After almost a century of mistrust and fratricide, you inspire Jews, Christians, and Muslims to take the path of reconciliation in the Middle East. We ask for your forgiveness, O God, yet we find it hard to forgive our past enemies. May your Words touch those who still stray in the wilderness of vengeful violence, forgetting your command to "forgive and overlook, till God accomplish his purpose; for God hath power over all things." Amen. (From Abdelwahab Hechiche, Tampa, Florida.)

Praying is vital, but praying is not enough. There's an old Latin phrase, *ora et labora*. It means believers are called to both prayer and labor, to both worship activity and actions in the world. We look now at our calling to work in the world of politics.

Public Policy Advocating

On the third *P*, the whole world seems to agree—that in the pursuit of Israel/Palestine peace, one party holds the key. It's not the government of Israel. It's not the Palestinian Authority. It's not the United Nations. It's the government of the United States of America. That has been the reality for more than three decades, a reality recognized by U.S. presidents from Lyndon Johnson on.

There are three reasons why the U.S. government holds the power to either birth or bar a just peace:

1. Its long-standing economic and military support, which makes Israel dependent on U.S. aid
2. Its ability as a veto holder to permit or prevent pertinent actions by the UN Security Council
3. Its status as the planet's sole superpower

The Central Role of the United States

In Samuel Lewis's review of U.S. diplomat Dennis Ross's *The Missing Peace*, Lewis wrote, "Sadly, the long history of this conflict supports Ross's basic argument: peace between Arabs and Israelis will come only with the active and sometimes intrusive support of U.S. diplomats, and especially of the U.S. president. So far, the current president [George W. Bush] has chosen not to heed this message. Until he (or his successor) does, comprehensive peace in the region will remain a receding horizon."[8]

The history of U.S. government pressure toward an Israel/Palestine peace is one of starts and stops. The fitful commitment of administrations, both Republican and Democrat, has been accompanied by continuing U.S. blockages of involvement by broader international bodies.

The UN Security Council has shown intense concern for peace and security in the Holy Land. And well it should, since almost sixty years ago, the UN called for creation of Israel and partitioned British Mandate Palestine into what was to be two independent states. But Security Council actions have had little impact on resolving the conflict. Israel routinely ignores such resolutions and keeps breaching international laws and regulations, including the 1949 Fourth Geneva Convention and the UN Charter. Specifically, Israel refuses compliance with Security Council resolutions 242 (1967) and 338 (1973), the foundation for all peace proposals over several decades.

Israel's blatant disregard for Security Council resolutions is undergirded by the almost unconditional support the country receives from the U.S. government. The United States has used its veto more than two dozen times since 1973 to kill resolutions on the conflict, usually claiming the resolutions are insufficiently balanced in what they say about the behavior of the two sides. Not only have U.S. vetoes prevented criticism of Israeli behavior (i.e., human-rights violations, collective punishment of Palestinians, settlements in occupied areas, home demolitions, and location of the separation wall). They have also prevented creation of a UN observer presence and on-site monitoring by an official international group.

A Double Standard

As Arab states in the Middle East are quick to point out, the United States applies a double standard when it comes to compliance with international agreements. The world knows, for example, that Israel has nuclear weapons, probably at least two hundred of them. But the specifics are not known because Israel's weapons-of-mass-destruction program has never been inspected by an international authority.

Israel has refused to accept any treaty regulating nuclear weapons, and the United States has not publicly pressed it to do so. In fact, the United States is in violation of its own law on this matter. It has legislation prohibiting financial aid to nations that develop nuclear weaponry outside of international scrutiny and control. Yet, as a writer in *Tikkun* magazine put it just prior to the 2003 U.S. invasion of Iraq:

> Israel has refused to sign any treaty regulating nuclear weapons, and has flouted other UN resolutions 69 times. The United States . . . gives Israel three billion dollars a year in aid, provides the bulk of its armaments and backs it against the UN, while trying to convince that same body that our convenient devil, Saddam Hussein, is a threat to peace because of uncontrollable development of weapons of mass destruction.[9]

Is it any wonder we Americans are viewed as hypocritical and two-faced throughout the region? That we have a double standard, one for Arab nations and one for Israel? The *Tikkun* article concluded with the rhetorical "Why do they hate us?"

The United States presents itself as an evenhanded broker of efforts toward peace between Palestine and Israel. Yet most of the world sees us rather as the prime enabler of Israel's continued military occupation of another people, with massive financial and arms support and shielding of Israel from global sanctions.

America's bipartisan 9/11 Commission, in its 2004 report about the 2001 terrorist attacks on New York City and Washington, D.C., cited as a central motivating factor for the attacks Arab anger at U.S. Middle East policies:

> Right or wrong, it is simply a fact that American policy regarding the Israeli-Palestinian conflict and American actions in Iraq are dominant staples of popular commentary across the Arab and Muslim world. That does not mean U.S. choices have been wrong. It means those choices must be integrated with America's message of opportunity to the Arab and Muslim world. Neither Israel nor the new Iraq will be safer if worldwide Islamist terrorism grows stronger.[10]

The Call to Citizens

In a citizens' democracy, all of voting age bear responsibility for their government's policies, domestic and foreign. We contribute, by our voices or by our silence, to what emerges as U.S. policy for the Middle East. So what precisely should we be voicing to our government representatives?

The main points regarding Israel and Palestine for which U.S. Christians should seek U.S. policy support are well known. They are what many studies and actions seeking peace, including those of both our government and the United Nations, have recommended.

There have been, since 1969, at least a dozen specific peace initiatives from either U.S. or international sources. These include the Rogers Plan (1969), the Scranton Mission on behalf of President Nixon (1970), Egyptian President Sadat's land-for-peace mutual recognition proposal (1971), President Carter's call for a Geneva international conference (1977), Saudi King Fahd's peace offer (1981), the Reagan Plan (1982), the Shultz Plan (1988), the Baker Plan (1989), a continuation of Clinton's Camp David negotiations at Taba (2001), the Saudi peace proposal on behalf of the Arab League (2002), the Quartet's road map (2003), and the unofficial Geneva Accord (2003).

And don't forget the 1993 Oslo Accords. They fell apart after the 1995 assassination of Yitzhak Rabin and the return to power in Israel of right-wing political forces. But they achieved two milestones: Israeli acceptance of a Palestinian Authority and Palestinian recognition of Israel's right to a secure existence.

These initiatives have generally been welcomed by Palestinians but entered only reluctantly and with qualifications by various Israeli governments. The initiatives have repeated essentially what UN Resolution 242 (November 22, 1967) called for. Its key provisions are:

- "Withdrawal of Israel armed forces from territories occupied in the recent conflict"
- "Termination of all claims or states of belligerency and respect for and acknowledgment of the sovereignty, territorial integrity and political independence of every state in the area and their right to live in peace within secure and recognized boundaries free from threats or acts of force"
- "A just settlement of the refugee problem"

Stances of Eight Presidencies
Direct U.S. government involvement with the conflict has a history of almost forty years. Here is a quick survey of stances and actions by presidential administrations since the 1967 war, with particular attention to Israel's occupation of Palestinian territory.

- *Johnson Administration:* "[Israel's government] is aware of our continuing concern that nothing be done in the occupied areas which might prejudice the search for a peace settlement. . . . Transfer of civilians to occupied areas, whether or not in settlements which are under military control, is contrary to Article 49 of the Geneva Convention" (State Department message to U.S. Embassy in Israel, quoted in Louis J. Smith, ed., *Foreign Relations of the United States, 1964–1968*, vol. 20, *Arab-Israeli Dispute 1967–1968*).

- *Nixon Administration:* "The application of Israeli law to occupied portions of [Jerusalem is] detrimental to our common interests in [Jerusalem]. The pattern of behavior authorized under the Geneva Convention and international law is clear: the occupier must maintain the occupied areas as intact and unaltered as possible, without interfering with the customary life of the area" (Charles Yost, U.S. Permanent Representative to the UN, Security Council, July 1, 1969).

- *Ford Administration:* "Substantial resettlement of the Israeli civilian population in occupied territories, including East Jerusalem, is illegal under the [Geneva] Convention. . . . Indeed, the presence of these settlements is seen by my government as an obstacle to the success of the negotiations for a just and final peace between Israel and its neighbors" (William Scranton, U.S. Ambassador to the UN, Security Council, March 23, 1976).

- *Carter Administration:* Jimmy Carter was the first president to make direct personal efforts toward peace between Israel and its neighbors. The Camp David negotiations he convened led to a peace agreement between Egypt and Israel in 1979. That agreement also called for an end to the occupation and creation of a Palestinian state living in peace alongside Israel.

- *Reagan Administration:* "Further settlement activity is in no way necessary for the security of Israel and only diminishes the confidence of the Arabs that a final outcome can be free and fairly negotiated" (Reagan Plan, September 1982).

- *George H. W. Bush Administration:* "My position is that the foreign policy of the United States says we do not believe there should be new settlements in the West Bank or in East Jerusalem. And I will conduct that policy as if it's firm, which it is" (George H. W. Bush, press conference, March 3, 1990).

- *Clinton Administration:* Bill Clinton was the second U.S. president to take an active personal role in seeking Israeli-Palestinian peace. His involvement sealed the Oslo Accords (Arafat-Rabin) on the White House lawn near his presidency's start (1993) and sought an agreement at Camp David (Arafat-Barak) up to its end in 2001. Both Oslo and the Camp David negotiations moved toward but failed to conclude a final peace. The Israel-Jordan peace treaty of 1994 also came during this period.

- *George W. Bush Administration:* "Israeli settlement activity in occupied territories must stop, and the occupation must end through withdrawal to secure and recognized boundaries, consistent with UN Resolutions 242 and 338" (Rose Garden address, April 4, 2002). Bush also initiated development of the road map to Israel-Palestine peace, issued in April 2003 by the Quartet (United States, European Union, Russia, and United Nations). Then, one year later, he departed from his road map—and from positions taken consistently by the seven previous U.S. administrations. In 2004 and 2005, Bush openly endorsed new policies pushed by Israeli Prime Minister Sharon. These unilateral, nonnegotiated plans included Israel's removing some 8,500 settlers from Gaza—with Israeli military presence still surrounding the strip and controlling access by sea and air. There were indications that, in return, Israel expected to be allowed to keep most West Bank settlements, to continue building the separation barrier inside Palestinian territory, and to refuse any return of Palestinian refugees to Israel proper.

Many observers see U.S. acceptance of Israel's unilateral "facts on the ground" activities as making creation of a separate Palestine highly unlikely. Certainly a Palestinian state that is viable—politically, economically, geographically—appeared by 2005 to have become a distant fantasy. Daniel Seidman, an Israeli attorney who monitors settlement activity in the Jerusalem area, has reflected on the probable result of U.S. blessing of recent Israeli behavior. The United States, he wrote, is guilty of "turning a blind eye to Israel's disingenuous representations regarding settlement expansion. Dovetailed with settlement activity, [the separation barrier] threatens to create a critical mass of political fact that further undermines the feasibility of the two-state solution."[11]

The Quartet's road map had called for establishment of a Palestinian state by 2005. Obviously, the 2005 deadline was not met, but as 2006 dawned, there was some hope that Israel and the Palestinian Authority would get back to the talking table.

What Can Christians Support?

What is the shape of a just peace between Israel and Palestine that Christians outside the Holy Land should be supporting? In my view, it is the vision enunciated by Churches for Middle East Peace (CMEP), a coalition of twenty-one U.S. Orthodox, Protestant, and Roman Catholic national policy offices.[12] CMEP seeks to convey to U.S. government officials (both the administration and Congress), as well as to the broader publics at home and abroad, the policies and priorities of its twenty-one member groups. The CMEP goals are expressed in this vision statement for its grassroots political education work:

> We are Christians called to express our concerns for peace in Israel and Palestine. We pray for peace in the Holy Land and urge our country's leaders to do all in their power to prepare the road for a long and lasting peace.
>
> We believe that one of the primary outcomes of peace negotiations in the Middle East must be a viable Palestinian state living in peace alongside the state of Israel. For a state of Palestine to be viable, all Israeli settlement activity in the Occupied Territories must cease.
>
> We believe in the vision of a shared Jerusalem as the heritage, hope and home of two peoples and three religions. Jerusalem should

be a shared, open city—a sign of peace and a symbol of reconciliation for the Abrahamic faiths.

We support a UN-sponsored, negotiated agreement for peace and the application of international law in all aspects of an Israeli-Palestinian-Arab peace process.

We strongly support a multinational presence of observers in the West Bank, Gaza Strip, and East Jerusalem as one immediate means of discouraging further violence between Palestinians and Israelis.

The CMEP vision statement captures what Christians today should be promoting if they desire justice and peace for the Holy Land. It contains what we're called to advocate, surely with elected officials, but also within our churches, in media communications, and in conversation with friends and neighbors.

Economic Pressures?

A related policy concern is U.S. economic and military aid to Israel, which annually has averaged $3 billion for almost three decades. Many advocates believe this aid package, by far our largest to any one country, gives our government superb leveraging opportunity with Israel. Israel has obviously become dependent on this aid. It is granted basically without conditions attached; Israel is not to spend it beyond the Green Line, but it clearly frees up other funds from Israel's treasury for subsidizing settlements and building settler-only roads and the security barrier inside Palestinian territory.

Even though given in violation of U.S. law, which forbids aid to countries that develop nuclear weapons outside international control, U.S. aid to Israel won't be ended or reduced much any time soon. But, if Congress would agree, the aid could at least carry specific peace-pursuing conditions, such as Israel returning to serious negotiations with Palestinians, ending all settlement activity on Palestinian land, situating the separation barrier on the 1967 border rather than inside Palestinian territory, and so forth.

Some advocates of change in Israel's behavior see private-sector economic tactics as the best way to go. They cite the example of South Africa in the 1980s, when worldwide economic pressures helped to bring down the apartheid system. The economic-pressure advocates promote withdrawing funds from multinational companies that benefit from Israel's occupation of Palestinian territory and boycotting products in international trade that are made in illegal Israeli settlements in Palestine.

The Presbyterian Church (U.S.A.) was the first North American denomination to take an official action that could lead to divestment from U.S. corporations that profit from Israel's occupation policies. Its general assembly voted (in summer 2004) to initiate "a process of phased selective divestment in multilateral corporations operating in Israel." No divesting can be done by the Presbyterians, however, unless its 2006 general assembly gives approval. In August 2005 the Presbyterians identified—for dialogue, shareholder resolutions, and "as a last resort" divestment—four U.S. companies that provide goods/services to the Israeli military and one that has allegedly dealt with Palestinian extremist groups.

The United Church of Christ, at its general synod in July 2005, adopted a policy on "Use of Economic Leverage in Promoting Peace in the Middle East." It asks that national agencies of the church, congregations, and members "use economic leverage, including, but not limited to: advocating the reallocation of U.S. foreign aid so that the militarization of the Middle East is constrained; making positive contributions to groups and partners committed to the non-violent resolution of the conflict; challenging the practices of corporations that gain from the continuation of the conflict; and divesting from those companies that refuse to change their practices of gain from the perpetuation of violence, including the Occupation."

The Evangelical Lutheran Church in America at its Churchwide Assembly in August 2005 adopted a campaign titled "Peace Not Walls: Stand for Justice in the Holy Land." One feature of the campaign deals with responsible stewarding of financial resources by the church and its members. It builds on a "Churchwide Strategy for ELCA Engagement in Israel and Palestine"

adopted by the ELCA's national Church Council in April 2005.
While not explicitly mentioning "divestment," that strategy
urges both members and church organizations to make invest-
ment decisions "with concern for their impact on the lives of all
Holy Land peoples who suffer from the ongoing conflict." The
strategy document further urges "consumer decisions that favor
support to those in greatest need (e.g., Palestinian providers
as distinct from Israeli settlers on Palestinian territory)." Also
advocated: that U.S. tax dollars go to both Palestinians and
Israelis "with equity and on condition that aid be used only for
economic growth and humanitarian needs." And the "Peace
Not Walls" adopting resolution notes that the ELCA Council
already in 2004 had asked for "an end to the construction of the
Israeli separation wall being built on Palestinian land."[13]

A boycott of products made by Israeli settlements on Palestinian territory has also received official support from the
governments of the European Union. The Israeli peace group,
Gush Shalom, promotes this boycott worldwide. For details, go
to http://gush-shalom.org and click on "boycott list of settlement products."

Tri-Faith Leaders' Initiative

Alongside CMEP, another faith-based group doing advocacy on
the Holy Land is the National Interreligious Initiative for Peace
in the Middle East. It unites top leaders of the three monotheistic faith traditions—Christian, Jewish, and Muslim—in seeking
to influence U.S. government behavior. These heads of religious
bodies promote vigorous engagement by the U.S. government,
including appointment of a special envoy with authority.

When it was publicly announced in December 2003, many
hailed the Interreligious Initiative as a true breakthrough
because of the group's diverse composition and its agreement
on proposals of substance. The religion columnist of the *New
York Times* wrote, "Given the range in this group and some very
real theological and political divisions among the members, [its
public statement] was remarkably specific and substantive."[14]

The group presses "12 urgent steps for peace," four to be taken by Israel, four by the Palestinian Authority, and four by the United States in coordination with the Quartet. The Christian-Jewish-Muslim coalition continues seeking opportunities for dialogue with top U.S. government officials. Parallel tri-faith initiatives are being organized in several regions of the country. The Web site of the national group is www.walktheroadtopeace.org.

Do leaders of the faith communities have a central role in bringing about justice and peace for the Holy Land? Exactly so, says the Lutheran leader there, Bishop Munib Younan. The leader of the Evangelical Lutheran Church in Jordan and the Holy Land told the council of the Lutheran World Federation that church leaders must join with Jewish and Muslim leaders in taking responsibility for achieving a just peace. Speaking on August 30, 2005, at Jerusalem's Lutheran Church of the Redeemer to an overflow crowd that included other Holy Land Christian leaders plus members of the local Islamic and Jewish communities, Bishop Younan said:

> If world leaders and politicians cannot make [peace and justice for Israelis and Palestinians] a reality, and if they cannot get out of their narrow national interests and see the human suffering and hear the prayers of both, then the church locally and globally must more proactively assume its responsibility with people of good conscience and courage from Judaism and Islam. . . . It is possible when people come to see that the security of Israel is dependent on freedom and justice for Palestinians and, simultaneously, freedom and justice for Palestinians is dependent on the security of Israel. This formula seeks true peace and healing for both peoples, but at the same time allows both to live in their own viable states according to the international standards of justice, equality, and equitable sharing of resources.

A New Time?

The year 2005 brought us to possibly a new period in the U.S.-Israel-Palestine equation. The Bush administration had entered its second term, and President Bush no longer needed to worry about reelection support from either the Christian Right or the Jewish lobby. Moreover, the Arafat era was over.

No longer could Israel's government say, "Arafat is not a worthy partner for peace talks." Of course, the Israeli authorities can invoke a similar dismissal, whenever they wish, regarding any Palestinian leadership. But both President Bush and Prime Minister Sharon have at least met with Palestinian President Mahmoud Abbas. That symbolizes some progress, since neither would even meet with Yasser Arafat.

An abundance of Israeli foot-dragging has marked peace processes for decades. And it continues to be clear that Israel gets serious about peace negotiations only when the United States insists on it. As President Bush began his second term, a conservative writer speculated skeptically on the possibility of Bush balance regarding Israel and Palestine:

> Neoconservatism now encompasses much more than Israel-obsessed intellectuals and policy insiders. The Bush foreign policy also surfs on deep currents within the Christian Right, some of which see unqualified support of Israel as part of a godly plan to bring about Armageddon and the future kingdom of Christ. These two strands of Jewish and Christian extremism build on one another in the Bush presidency—and President Bush has given not the slightest indication he would restrain either in a second term.[15]

As this is written (late 2005), it is still unclear whether prospects for a just peace are enhanced or diminished by having President Bush located in a second term—or by the emergence of new Palestinian leadership. One thing clearly has not changed: a key part of Christian vocation remains that we, in the United States especially, use citizenship power to demand that our elected officials be a help rather than a hindrance to justice and peace in that land named Holy. And how we Christians and our churches use our economic power is an equally important part of the peacemaking vocation to which God calls us.

Pilgrimage Making/Offering Presence

The practice of nonresidents visiting the Holy Land has a long, hallowed, and (for those residing there) often painful history. For centuries, Christians have made treks to the Mediterranean's southeast corner. Many have wanted only to deepen their faith by placing their feet on soil where they believed the feet of Jesus also stepped. But pilgrims' feet have not always trod gently—or peacefully.

Both Muslims and Eastern Christians were hurt deeply by the ravages Western powers perpetrated, in the name of the Christian God, a millennium ago. The memory of the Crusades, when armies came from Europe to conquer the land in the name of Christendom, still rankles throughout the region. Indeed, many view carving out land for Israel in 1947–48 as simply a continuation of Crusader mentality on the part of powerful Western nations.

Politicizing Tourism

After the Al-Aqsa Intifada erupted in September 2000, conventional tourism in the Holy Land dropped dramatically. Church groups that still go are likely to limit their visits to Israel proper, not venturing into occupied Palestinian areas, such as Bethlehem. For many, getting through Israeli military checkpoints and roadblocks (sixty in the Bethlehem area alone) makes these trips not worth the hassle and an inevitable waste of time. A 2004 survey reported that, from a monthly average four years earlier of one hundred thousand tourists, Bethlehem visitors had dropped to five thousand a month. Bethlehem's twelve hotels, all owned by Christians, had closed.

"A dead city" Bethlehem was called by Bernard Sabella, a Catholic who teaches at Bethlehem University. He said the emptiness he feels when walking through Bethlehem's Church of the Nativity compound totally contradicts the theology behind the nativity and God's incarnation.

Even the relatively few visits by Christians to this land have been politicized. Most Christians arrive with a distinct political viewpoint and a program that has at least some political content. That is, organized church groups typically come with plans, somewhere on their agenda, to show support for particular players in the Israel/Palestine conflict. One can still make pilgrimage with a sole motive of visiting biblical sites and renewing faith perspectives. Even then, it's rare for groups not to bring along a viewpoint on the conflict.

Some groups, identified as Christian Zionists, go explicitly to stand with Israeli factions that insist all the land, from the sea to the river, belongs to Israel by divine directive (see chapter 3). Others go to show solidarity with Palestinians struggling for freedom and the right to sovereignty over part of that land. Still others go mainly to meet with and learn from indigenous efforts, both Israeli and Palestinian, to work for peace, security, and human rights for all.

Visiting Christians who want to show solidarity with Palestinians and who meet with peace and human-rights groups usually spend time with local Christians, both in Israel and in occupied Palestine. Visitors who identify as Christian Zionists rarely meet with indigenous Christians, which is deeply offensive to local believers.

Palestinian Christians Are Off-Limits

The Reverend Mitri Raheb, pastor of Christmas Lutheran Church in Bethlehem, told a *Minneapolis Star Tribune* reporter why Christian Zionists seldom meet with Palestinian Christians. "They regard us as not true Christians," he said. In the same article JoAnn Magnuson, national communication director of Bridges for Peace, noted that groups sent by her agency once spent time with Palestinian Christians but stopped doing so because "the rhetoric they were dealing with was so anti-Israel."[16]

Magnuson, who calls herself a Christian Zionist, told the Minneapolis paper that by mid-2003 she had been to Israel fifty-two times. Her organization arranges visits for church people of conservative-evangelical persuasion. Bridges for Peace states these specific objectives (with no mention of Palestinians or of Christians anywhere in the Holy Land):

> To educate and equip Christians to identify with Israel, the Jewish people, and the biblical/Hebraic foundation of our Christian faith.
>
> To communicate Christian perspectives to the attention of Israeli leaders and the Jewish community-at-large.
>
> To counter anti-Semitism worldwide and support Israel's divine God-given right to exist in her God-given land.[17]

Another U.S.-based group organizing visits to Israel is Messianic Messages. Its Web site (www.messianicmessages.com) says it is "a ministry devoted to teaching the predominantly Gentile Church about her Jewish heritage and to instilling a love and concern for the land and people of Israel." Its trips include visits to the office of Christian Friends of Israel in Jerusalem and contact with Israeli Jews. Meeting Palestinians, Christian or otherwise, is no part of the program.

And for decades, North American Jewish agencies have, along with the Israeli government, offered subsidized tours in Israel for Christian clergy. Itineraries for these visits include no contact with Palestinians (except for maybe a shopkeeper or two). The sole entry into occupied territory may be a bus visit to Bethlehem for about an hour. Only Israeli-government-approved guides lead such tours.

Tour Alternatives

A development in recent years has been the intentional planning of visits for church groups that are called "alternative" or "authentic" tours. Usually ten days to two weeks in length, such trips typically have the following features:

- Include both the Palestinian West Bank and Israel proper
- Use Palestinian providers of services (guides, hotels, restaurants)
- Plan meetings with Palestinians as well as Israelis
- Schedule worship with local Christians and visits to church-sponsored humanitarian ministries

Connecting with indigenous Christians should be central to pilgrimage by Christians from overseas. But sadly, it has become a rarity, even for visitors to Jerusalem itself. Marc Ellis, an American Jewish theologian, describes what Holy City visits have become for most Christians, with Israel controlling Jerusalem's heart and displacing its former Palestinian residents:

> What should be an evolving religious sensibility rooted in faith, culture, and politics is [now visiting a shrine] to an ancient reality unconnected with contemporary life. Orthodox Jews increasingly determine the pattern of life in Jerusalem, and Christian pilgrims from the West celebrate their festivals as if there are no indigenous Christians in the land.[18]

A book designed to help visiting Christians have meaningful contact with local Christians is *Living Stones Pilgrimage: With the Christians of the Holy Land.* "Its purpose is to transform Christian visitors into pilgrims by luring them off the tourist track into the company of Palestinian fellow-believers who trace their roots to the disciples of Jesus," says Father Jerome Murphy-O'Connor, a scholar at Jerusalem's École Biblique. "It is more concerned with people than places."[19]

Some U.S. tour agencies specialize in linking Christian visitors with local Christians. One that is especially well respected for the quality and sensitivity of its work—both with church or school groups in North America and with Palestinian service providers—is Group Travel Directors, based in suburban Minneapolis. Its Web site is www.gtd.org.

Upon Arrival

The political nature of travel in the Holy Land does not end with itinerary planning. Israel controls access to the entire land, Israel proper and also the Palestinian territories it occupies and surrounds militarily. Israel has, quite understandably, a concern for security and is therefore exceedingly careful about who it allows to enter. It is especially suspicious about visitors who come with ideas that Israel considers politically suspect. Touring groups and individuals undergo intense scrutiny and questioning when seeking to enter.

Most visitors arrive via Israel's Ben Gurion International Airport, near Tel Aviv. Some enter by land crossings from Jordan or Egypt. All entry points are tightly controlled. Security officials ask about the visit's purpose, where the visitor will be going and where lodging is planned, whether meetings with Palestinians are scheduled, and so on. With groups, a copy of the daily program may be requested.

When departing as well, especially via Tel Aviv's Ben Gurion airport, the visitor may expect rigorous questioning. Where did you go? Why were you here? With whom did you meet? Bags are examined with scrupulous care. Sometimes printed material that suggests political content is confiscated.

Even the maps given to visitors are political statements. The "Pilgrim's Map of the Holy Land," issued by Israel's Ministry of Tourism, does not show the Green Line, the internationally recognized boundary between Israel and Palestinian territory. The 2001 edition designates with color blocks those areas where, under the Oslo agreement, Palestinians had responsibility for "civil affairs, internal security, and public order." But overall the map has the West Bank, East Jerusalem, Gaza Strip, Golan Heights, and Israel proper all together without distinction. The whole is circled by a line marked "international boundary," obviously suggesting that the entirety is Israel.

Palestinians have their own maps. One from 2002 shows the West Bank, East Jerusalem, and Gaza as part of Palestine. It shows locations of Israeli settlements on Palestinian territory. It includes the site of "Gaza International Airport," provided for under the Oslo agreement in the mid-1990s but destroyed by Israel in 2000 and not operating since. All adjacent areas of Israel proper, with cities and towns, show on this "Map of Palestine." But the name *Israel?* That appears nowhere.

Global Church Presence

This land has had presence by expressions of the global church for 1,700 years. It's been true since Helena, mother of Roman Emperor Constantine, visited (326 CE) and decided to provide for construction of churches in two places: Bethlehem, Jesus' birthplace, and Jerusalem, where he was crucified.

In the centuries since, the church's international presence has continued without ceasing, in a variety of forms. For example, the Franciscan Order of the Roman Catholic Church cares for most biblical sites important to Christians. For some Christian traditions, leaders come from outside. In addition, there are workers in the many educational, medical, and other humanitarian programs supported by the worldwide church.

People coming from other countries to help operate these ministries are one category of global church presence in this land. Many stay for years, even decades. For some Christian expatriates, an entire lifework is spent in this land.

A second category of visitors also consists of workers, but for a shorter term, often as unpaid volunteers. They normally sign on for several months or perhaps a year, and serve at schools, with hospitals, in church offices, or with peace and human-rights organizations.

Christians from elsewhere in the world now fill a role that has been denied to representatives of governments: that of a multinational body of observer-monitors. Proposals for such a presence have consistently been opposed by Israel and, when advanced in the UN Security Council, vetoed by the United States at Israel's behest. Today, two specific church efforts provide a peace-seeking presence from within the global civil community:

1. *Ecumenical Accompaniment Programme in Palestine and Israel*— Organized by the World Council of Churches in consultation with Palestinian churches, this program was launched in mid-2002. Christians from around the world serve for three-month periods. More than two hundred accompaniers from thirteen countries served during the program's first three years. Accompaniers monitor and report violations of international humanitarian law, support acts of nonviolent resistance alongside Christian and Muslim Palestinians and Israeli peace activists, offer protection through their presence, engage in public-policy advocacy, and stand in solidarity with the churches and all who struggle against the occupation. Web site: www.eappi.org.

2. *Christian Peacemaker Teams*—A program seeking to sustain a nonviolent presence in several of the world's trouble spots, CPT is supported by U.S. denominations of the historic pacifist tradition. Its formation arose "from scriptural encouragement for creative public ministry and enemy-loving in the spirit of Jesus. Christians who refuse to kill in conflict situations bring an important gift to the table." CPT has had a team in Hebron, West Bank, since 1995. Full-time team members typically serve a three-year term. Team reservists provide support for periods of two weeks to two months. Web site: www.cpt.org.

CPT volunteers pledge never to use violence, but that doesn't always protect them from receiving violence. In September 2004, two team members in Hebron, while escorting Palestinian children to school, were viciously attacked by Israeli settlers. Kim Lamberty, an American who was injured, said later to an Israeli newspaper reporter, "The attackers wanted to intimidate us, frighten us, force us into leaving, but it won't happen. Because if they escalate the violence, we'll escalate the nonviolence."[20]

In the same Israeli paper, another team member commented on CPT's commitment to resist violence, whatever its source. Diane Jenzen, a Mennonite from Canada, noted that CPTers "have ridden on Jerusalem buses to deter suicide bombers [and] stood in the way of a Palestinian who tried to stab [an Israeli] soldier."

Going to Gain Hope

A third category of Holy Land visitors are those going for a short time, typically ten to fourteen days. Even brief stays play a part in the process of accompanying presence with suffering fellow humans. Such visits also let us from abroad view firsthand the ministries of Christians under difficult circumstances[21] and, ironically, to learn hope from those living in situations that seem hopeless. Says Mitri Raheb, the Lutheran pastor in Bethlehem:

> Some visitors have. . . wanted to see us as mere victims, hopeless and helpless. But that attitude victimizes us, the victims. Although we are victims, we are not *only* victims. We have fears and tears, but we have hopes and dreams, too. We aren't just helpless people, nor are we a hopeless case . . . . It's important for us to hear our visitors tell us that what they've seen here has given them hope, strength, and commitment to go back and make a change.[22]

Whether for two weeks or two decades, why would anyone plan a visit to the Holy Land? Given the difficulty of getting in and getting around, why would one bother to go? Given the concern about physical danger, why would one choose to be there? Given the fact that the entire area has been under a U.S. State Department travel advisory since October 2000, shortly after the outbreak of the Al-Aqsa Intifada, why would a U.S. citizen even risk it? Unlike travel to Cuba, which is severely restricted by U.S. law, American citizens are not legally barred from going to Israel/Palestine. But the U.S. government does want citizens to know about risks anywhere, and its warning against Holy Land travel is now in its sixth year without a break.[23]

Is there danger of physical harm? Yes, but in my experience it's tiny. No tour groups in Israel/Palestine have ever been targeted by violent acts—though some elsewhere in the world have been. And while a few internationals working for Palestinian rights have died as a result of Israel's military occupation (the American Rachel Corrie in 2003 among them), the closest to harm's way for conventional tourists is to have young Israeli soldiers carelessly waving guns toward them at checkpoints.

Between 1997 and 2005, I've led five groups on Holy Land visits. Most of the nearly one hundred who went with me had some apprehension in advance of trips. But without exception, participants have been able to say that, once on the ground in Israel and Palestine, they felt as safe as back home. It helps that we always take care to follow the counsel of those hosting us, concerning where to go when.

And the hospitality of all with whom we meet, Palestinians and Israelis alike, exhibits the traditional warmth and welcome for which Middle East cultures are deservedly known. A visitor from the United States could expect that Palestinians might be hostile to any American, given our government's long-standing tilt toward the Israeli government. Palestinians almost universally see U.S. policy as unfair, slighting Palestinian interests. But Palestinians don't generally hold U.S. visitors responsible for U.S. national policy. They like to say, "We despise your government's behavior, but we like you Americans as people."

Going to Receive

There are basically two reasons for Christians to visit the Holy Land, even—and especially—in times of stress: for what we can receive, for what we can give. This is what we receive, beyond the benefits of growing spiritually via pilgrimage to the land where the Christian faith was born:

- Christians visiting today receive an understanding of the realities of the conflict that is firsthand and face-to-face. We learn that the struggle is not finally about win-lose ideologies or political theologies. It's about ordinary human beings seeking a way for two peoples and three faith traditions to live together in harmony and mutual respect.

• Christians visiting today gain a more balanced, more nuanced awareness of the diversity within both Palestinian and Israeli peoples. These visitors are then able to get beyond stereotypes: that all Palestinians support suicide bombing of Israelis, or that all Israelis support continuing oppression of Palestinians. At the same time, visitors get in the gut a sense that there is a common, profoundly unifying thread that links solid majorities of both peoples—the hunger for an end to violence, for a peaceful coexistence, for the simple option of normalcy in their everyday living.

• Most important, as Mitri Raheb says, Christians visiting today receive the gift of hope. We learn from our hosts that there remains hope for a peaceful and just future in this land, for all who dwell there. Many visiting Christians, who arrived carrying a load of despair concerning the conflict, report after their visit that they were turned around by what they experienced. They did not bring hope with them. They received it while there and, in what is often called a life-changing experience, took that hope home with them.

Often, writes Pastor Raheb, members of visiting groups will say, "We came here aiming to give you hope and to strengthen you in your struggle, but we leave . . . having received more than we brought with us. It is you who give us hope, and it is you . . . who strengthen us."[24] This new hope that visitors receive should lead us to think and act differently once we arrive home. Raheb writes:

A hopeful vision is . . . important for American and European Christians. Not because they need to be pro-Palestinian, but because they need to stop being spectators in their own country. We are not asking for more statements on the Middle East. We are asking for action—not only for our sake, but also for their own sake. . . . Citizens of these countries must care that their money be spent not to subsidize the Israeli occupation but to create a just peace in the region. . . . Christian hope holds firm that it's never too late for faith in action and for acts of compassion. Christian hope does not surrender to the forces of death and despair but challenges them.[25]

Going to Give

As Holy Land visitors, we receive much, but we have much to give, too. What we give by visiting Israel and Palestine in these days is, at bottom, the gift of our presence. That presence brings with it the priceless gift of accompaniment, simply being with and standing with and working with others in their time of special need. It gives both Palestinians and Israelis a crucial learning: the discovery that there are Christians elsewhere in the world who reject Christian Zionist ideology.

For those joining intentional accompaniment efforts, such as Christian Peacemaker Teams or Ecumenical Accompaniment, the contributions are obvious. When internationals are with Palestinians trying to pass military checkpoints or gates in the separation wall or harvesting olives, the Palestinians normally face less harassment from Israeli soldiers or from Israeli settlers near olive groves. When internationals work with Israeli peace and human-rights groups, such groups' actions have greater impact, both locally and globally.

The Christians who go to work in the Holy Land for the longer term bring specific skills and experience that meet needs. These expatriate workers are valuable contributors, both through ministries of the church in that land and through a variety of essential services operating under secular auspices.

And those who visit for only a week or two? We also give. We give in our willingness to listen and learn. We give in praying and worshiping with fellow believers. We give by showing beleaguered peoples that the rest of the world has not forgotten them. We give when offering assurances that we leave with new zeal to work back home for justice and peace in the land called holy.

Peace Hopers to Peacemakers

We who go do indeed end our visits with new hope, but also with new commitment to be Holy Land peace seekers at home.

The Reverend Fuad Dagher is rector of Saint Paul's Episcopal Church in Shefar'Am, a community in Israel's Galilee between Nazareth and Haifa. He visited a sister congregation, Saint Anselm of Canterbury Episcopal Church in Garden Grove, California, in 2004. This Palestinian-Israeli priest stressed the usefulness of linking Christians in the Holy Land with Christians elsewhere. He spoke of the values for both parties in ongoing parish-to-parish relationships. Father Dagher then said those who would aid struggling Palestinian Christians should first "come and see." He elaborated with this word:

> The church in the West, I am sorry to say, has been silent for many years. Our Lord said, blessed are the peacemakers. He didn't say blessed are the peace-hopers. It is my task. It is your task. Speak up and try to be an instrument of God's peace. Not all Palestinians are terrorists. Come and visit us and see.[26]

When You Get Home

North Americans who spend time with Palestinians, whether it's measured in weeks or in years, do return home one day. And almost without exception, they speak of their time in that special space as life changing. What is different for them?

How they think about the Palestine/Israel reality, for starters. But they also act in different ways. It nearly always means some combination of commitments such as these:

- Sharing what they've learned by offering to speak in local churches and other forums
- Putting more energy into advocacy with government officials on U.S. Middle East policies
- Adding the quest for Holy Land justice and peace to their regular prayer agenda

- Giving media communication a more critical eye and ear, with new awareness of the story behind the story being told
- Asking home congregations to form ongoing links with Palestinian congregations
- Increasing significantly their financial support of church ministries in the Holy Land
- Urging friends and neighbors to see for themselves by visiting that land

Those Four *P*s

To conclude, we Christians who are concerned with the Holy Land have a calling. It's made up of four *P*s: Paying attention; Praying fervently; Public-policy advocating; Pilgrimage making.

May God bless us as we pursue this calling and give us the wisdom and strength to add to our calling a fifth *P*, that of Peace building—both for ourselves and for *all* the peoples of the land called Holy.

Pilgrims visiting Bethlehem's Church of the Nativity since 2000 have had little crowd pressure to deal with. Heading for the sanctuary built over the traditional site of Jesus' birth was this group of U.S. Christians on a 2005 visit.

Appendix

Whose Land Is It?

Ronald D. Witherup, S.S.

The view of Jerusalem from the Mount of Olives is one of the most impressive in the Holy Land. The first time I gazed upon the walls of the Old City (in 1992), I got goose bumps. My dream of finally visiting the land where Jesus had lived and walked had come true. But it did not take long for reality to intrude. Blaring sirens halted my quiet reflection. As majestic as the scene before me was, this was nevertheless a contemporary human battleground.

An age-old tug-of-war continues in and around the city. And at the heart of the dispute is the question "Whose land is it?" My aim here is to offer a personal reflection on that question, especially from the biblical point of view. The situation is much too complex to treat thoroughly here, but we can set forth a basic approach. Much of the Israeli-Palestinian conflict involves disputes over the land. Various parties beyond these two groups weigh in on the question, often using biblical warrants to justify their perspectives. While I do not think biblical data alone can decide the question, thoughtful reflection on them might issue us a note of caution and place the question in proper perspective.

Terminology and the Land

The land is a major theme in the Old Testament. Several scholarly studies have been devoted to the subject, and I cannot rehearse all the research here.[1] My goal is simply to explore the essential biblical perspectives on the land that might shed light on what is proper or improper use of the Bible in addressing the question. As has been true for ages, people of all stripes invoke the Bible as a kind of sanction for one position or another. Indeed, the Bible was collated over such an extensive time period and in such varying circumstances that virtually any position can be defended on the basis of one passage or another. Whether this is defensible from a contemporary scholarly perspective is another matter.

Let's look first at some of the passages most commonly used with regard to the Land of Israel. At the outset, I emphasize that even basic terminology can be misleading. The land at the center of the dispute can be called Israel or Palestine or the Holy Land—depending on your viewpoint. While "Holy Land"[2] reflects basically a Christian orientation (expressing this area's connection to the life, ministry, death, and resurrection of Jesus), the other two terms also have validity from different points of view.

"Israel" is the name of the ancient kingdom that King David ruled over, once he united the twelve tribes. It also refers to the northern kingdom after the death of Solomon (922 BCE), which was distinct from the southern kingdom, Judah. But Israel also now designates the modern state created by the United Nations in 1947–48, in the wake of the Holocaust and World War II. Pious Jews honor "the Land of Israel" (*'Eretz Israel*; cf. 1 Samuel 13:19) as a Jewish homeland that fulfills the expectations of the [Hebrew Scripture] promises that God would create a safe place for the people of the covenant.

"Palestine" simultaneously names an area that once encompassed the Roman province of Judea but also designated a wider region in the eastern Mediterranean. Now the name applies to a

fledgling and hoped-for future homeland for modern Arabs who
call themselves Palestinians and who seek an independent state
alongside the state of Israel.

Bandying these titles about can get one into tight situations.
In using a specific term, one can be making a political statement or claim. As a Christian, I prefer to refer to the modern
state of Israel and the adjacent Palestinian territories (the West
Bank, Gaza, and East Jerusalem) as the Holy Land. I feel it is the
most neutral term. Although the term is seen to be of Christian
origin, the reality of Jerusalem as a city deemed holy by three
faiths (Judaism, Christianity, and Islam) gives some legitimation
to using the generic "Holy Land" for the entire area.

The Old Testament Perspective

What is the biblical testimony about the land?[3] I will summarize
the data and then offer some critical remarks based upon the
current state of scholarship.

To begin with, even a cursory reading of the Bible shows that
God (the God of Israel—Yahweh) promised a land to Abram,
the father of Judaism, as part of the covenant between them. At
God's direction, Abram sets out from his own homeland, Ur of
the Chaldeans, to journey to the land of Canaan. But, the text
proceeds, "At that time the Canaanites were in the land. Then
the Lord appeared to Abram, and said, 'To your offspring I will
give this land'" (Genesis 12:6b-7; cf. 15:18-21; 17:5-8). God
repeats this promise to Isaac and Jacob, thus reaffirming to the
great triumvirate of patriarchs the promise of a land to this chosen people (cf. Genesis 26:3-4; 28:13-15; 50:24).[4]

Subsequent Old Testament books pick up on these promises, especially Exodus, Deuteronomy, and Joshua. Heroes like
Moses and Joshua are portrayed as leading the chosen people to
the "promised land" in fulfillment of God's covenant. This land
is sometimes described as flowing with "milk and honey," signs
of prosperity and peace (Exodus 3:8, 17; 13:5). This scenario
also includes the annihilation of the various peoples who inhabit

the land (Deuteronomy 7:1-11; 20:16-18). This is part of a complex reality called the *herem* or "sacred ban" in which everything opposed to God and standing in the way of the chosen people is to be destroyed. This is both to honor God fully and to prevent self-service looting for one's own benefit. Although this aspect of the biblical faith strikes modern ears offensively, it was part of the culture at the time and is deeply embedded in the Old Testament understanding of God as a divine warrior who is out to protect his people.

Interpreting the Biblical Perspective

What is one to make of these data? Scholars point to several problematic aspects of the Old Testament scenario:

A first problem is that the historicity of the patriarchal narratives is highly questionable, at least in the details. While some aspects of the narratives in Genesis are consonant with what is known from outside sources, other details are not. The name *Chaldeans*, for instance, is anachronistic; they did not come into existence until around the ninth century BCE, centuries after Abram's time. There is no guarantee that the events narrated concerning the time of the patriarchs—eighteenth century BCE—are actually a record of that time. In fact, there are clear indications that later materials have crept into the narrative and reflect an interpretation of the narrated events from later perspectives. This should not surprise us. The Old Testament in written form only began to come into existence in the tenth century BCE, around the time of King David, and continued down to the second century BCE. Later writers often reworked the traditions, especially after the Exile (sixth century BCE), to reflect their own theological viewpoint. This fact is simply an acknowledgment that the Bible is both history and theology. There are multiple layers of both embedded in the biblical story. Sorting the one from the other is a tenuous task, and with the land traditions can be especially daunting. Moreover, the texts bear witness to historical developments over a long period of time, such as the sociological change from a nomadic society to one that was more agricultural, settled, and urban.

Second, there is implicit acknowledgment in the Old Testament that the land did not belong to God's chosen people originally, but becomes theirs via the covenant with Yahweh. It is, in fact, the land of the Canaanites, among others (e.g., Kenites, Kennizites, Amorites, Jebusites; cf. Genesis 12:5; 15:19; 23:2; Exodus 3:17). There were, obviously, indigenous peoples in the land when the Israelites arrived. Nowhere does the Bible address this issue from an ethical or moral viewpoint. Rather, the theological perspective dominates the Old Testament, in which the land is "promised" to Israel.

Third, archaeological evidence, which at times can be used to show the historical accuracy of ancient biblical texts, sometimes demonstrates the opposite. Most glaring, for instance, is the biblical description of the fall of such towns as Jericho or Ai. Archaeological digs have shown that these cities did not exist as walled cities in the time of the patriarchs, and indeed there is no evidence of massive destruction of these cities in the time period described by the Bible. Moreover, many scholars now see evidence of a gradual, peaceful settlement of the land over time, the Israelites intermingling with the native populations, in contrast to the biblical portrait of a warlike conquest described in Joshua and Judges.

Fourth, even the extent of the land of Israel in biblical times, usually designated as "the land of Canaan," is uncertain. The common formula invoked to note the boundaries of ancient Israel is "from Dan to Beersheba" (Judges 20:1; 1 Samuel 3:20; 2 Samuel 17:11), but scholars know the boundaries changed and were fairly fluid throughout the entire Old Testament period. One text (Genesis 15:18), which seems hyperbolic, speaks of the scope of the land as extending from the Nile to the Euphrates, thus from Egypt to modern Iraq! The extension of the boundaries from Dan in the north to Beersheba in the south usually refers to land west of the Jordan River, but does not include the Mediterranean coastal region.

Finally, the biblical perspective is sometimes clouded by political agendas and is influenced heavily by literalistic interpretations. In particular, radical religious Zionists have used the biblical data as an absolute warrant for the forceful taking of land in our day, on the assumption that these ancient texts justify modern behavior. In a strange twist, some fundamentalist Christians support this position, albeit for their own reasons. They believe God's kingdom will come fully only after the state of Israel is reestablished in its full biblical proportions and the Temple is restored. The complex history of intervening centuries plays no part in this simplistic reading of the Bible.

Confronting the Current Reality

The biblical perspective, then, cannot be followed in every detail as a kind of blueprint for the contemporary political situation in the Holy Land. We should acknowledge the perennial value of the Bible's teachings without asserting that the Bible applies directly to every ethical or political issue in our own time. This approach is both thoroughly Catholic and consistent with many other interpretive traditions, Protestant and Jewish included. In my judgment, the only place to begin with the land question is not with the Bible but with the facts of the present situation in the Holy Land. The situation "on the ground" is what we must now confront. There can be no going back to an idyllic, premodern vision. With this in mind, I offer three minimal elements of the current situation that must be acknowledged as the land issue is addressed:

1. Both peoples, Israelis and Palestinians, will have to learn to coexist peacefully. The land really belongs to both of them and must be shared. The state of Israel is a fact and has the right to exist in peace and security. There is no returning to a pre-1947 world. At the same time, the Palestinians have a right to exist as a nation. They must be guaranteed a fair, independent, viable, and contiguous state to call their own.

In addition, the resources of the land—such as water, so crucial in that desert climate—must be shared fairly.

2. The current Israeli practice of forcefully expanding settlements in Palestinian territories is wrong, morally and legally. It violates international law (both Geneva Conventions and UN resolutions). It also exacerbates the problem of preserving territory for a viable, independent Palestinian state. The facts are important to recall. More than two hundred settlements now exist in the occupied territories, and some four hundred thousand Israelis have crossed the internationally recognized borders to live in these new areas. When speaking with some of the Israeli settlers, many of whom are Jewish immigrants from other countries, including the United States, one hears that the settler movement is justified because of biblical promises.

3. Jerusalem remains a thorny problem, especially because of its unique status in the three great monotheistic faiths. The Holy See has repeatedly called for special consideration of Jerusalem. Internationally, Jerusalem is not recognized as the capital of Israel, despite Israel's 1967 unilateral declaration to that effect. Jerusalem must be preserved both as an entity where so many holy sites exist side by side and attract (when conflict subsides) many international visitors, and also as home to many diverse religious communities who have a right to preserve their homes and way of life.

Conclusion

As I mull the memories of my several Holy Land visits, I recall not just the various images of the fascinating places I visited. I recall also the many people I met and conversed with, both Palestinian and Jewish. The sense of fatalism and depression was at times almost overwhelming. Both sides have obvious love for the land, and both are struggling to preserve what they believe is a God-given right to possess it.

As John Paul II said on more than one occasion, what must be preserved is not only the Holy Land itself but human dignity. Human rights take precedence over ancient claims to the land. These two peoples who have common Semitic roots must strive harder to overcome their ancient prejudices and negotiate a fair and just resolution to the current crisis. The biblical tradition should not be used literalistically to justify a modern, political outcome. Violence only begets more violence; it cannot solve the problem.

Although I am not naive enough to believe the resolution will come easily or quickly, I do pray that we who stand on the sidelines show more willingness to help. I still gaze out over the Holy City of Jerusalem and let the psalmist's words flood over me: "Pray for the peace of Jerusalem: 'May they prosper who love you. Peace be within your walls'" (Psalm 122:6-7).

Resources

Books

Armstrong, Karen. *Jerusalem: One City, Three Faiths*. New York: Knopf, 1996. Tells how Jews, Christians, and Muslims have seen Jerusalem as their holy city and how three differing monotheistic traditions have shaped and scarred Jerusalem over several millennia. See also *Holy War: The Crusades and Their Impact on Today's World*, 2nd ed. (New York: Anchor, 2001).

Ateek, Naim. *Justice and Only Justice: A Palestinian Theology of Liberation*. Maryknoll, N.Y.: Orbis, 1989. An Anglican Palestinian articulates a liberation theology for Palestinian people based on principles of justice, peace, and nonviolence.

Ateek, Naim S., Marc H. Ellis, and Rosemary Radford Ruether, eds. *Faith and the Intifada: Palestinian Christian Voices*. Maryknoll, N.Y.: Orbis, 1992. A collection of nineteen essays by Palestinian Christians, with eight responses by internationals, in the context of the first Palestinian uprising. Much of the collection first appeared as papers given during a March 1990 international symposium on Palestinian liberation theology at Tantur, between Bethlehem and Jerusalem.

Avishai, Bernard. *The Tragedy of Zionism: Revolution and Democracy in the Land of Israel*. New York: Helios, 1985. Addresses questions such as these: Can Israel be a democratic state while discriminating against non-Jews (a fifth of its citizens are Palestinian Arabs)? Can Israel be a Jewish state without granting a privileged position to Jewish Orthodoxy? Avishai Margalit, in the *New York Review of Books*, describes Avishai as "not a foreign observer, but a pained insider."

Bailey, Betty Jane, and Allison Hilliard. *Living Stones Pilgrimage: With the Christians in the Holy Land*. Notre Dame, Ind.: University of Notre Dame

Press, 1999. Not your usual tourist manual, this guidebook seeks to help visiting Christians have meaningful contact with local Christians in Palestine and Israel.

Bailey, Betty Jane, and J. Martin Bailey. *Who Are the Christians in the Middle East?* Grand Rapids: Eerdmans, 2003. A useful survey of the diverse Christian communities in the region, from North Africa to Iran. The Baileys, U.S. United Church of Christ members, have spent many years working in the Middle East.

Bennis, Phyllis. *Understanding the Palestinian-Israeli Conflict: A Primer.* Onset, Mass.: Trans-Arab Research Institute, 2003. Provides clear analysis of the conflict from historical, political, and diplomatic perspectives. See also *Before and After: US Foreign Policy and the September 11th Crisis* (New York: Olive Branch, 2002).

Burge, Gary. *Whose Land? Whose Promise? What Christians Are Not Being Told about Israel.* Cleveland: Pilgrim, 2003. The author, president of Evangelicals for Middle East Understanding, explores biblical material that some evangelicals say gives Israel absolute right to all of the Holy Land. His conclusion: "The church cannot be entangled in a political agenda that destroys people and pursues injustice." See also *Who Are God's People in the Middle East?* (Grand Rapids: Zondervan, 1993).

Carey, Roane, and Jonathan Shainin, eds. *The Other Israel: Voices of Refusal and Dissent.* New York: New Press, 2002. With a foreword by historian and commentator Tom Segev, this small book collects several short essays from Jewish Israeli authors critical of Israeli policies and the future of Zionism. Contributors include Ze'ev Sternhell, Jeff Halper, Amira Hass, Uri Avnery, and Ilan Pappe.

Chacour, Elias, with Mary E. Jensen. *We Belong to the Land.* New York: HarperCollins, 1990. The story of a Palestinian Israeli citizen who works for peace and reconciliation between two peoples living on the same land. Chacour is a Melkite Catholic priest serving in Galilee. Jensen is a U.S. Lutheran pastor who has served as communication assistant to Jerusalem's Lutheran bishop. See also *Blood Brothers* (Grand Rapids: Zondervan, 1982).

Chapman, Colin. *Whose Promised Land? The Continuing Crisis over Israel and Palestine.* Grand Rapids: Baker, 2002. This volume is a veritable sourcebook of diverse perspectives on the Palestinian-Israeli conflict. Chapman explores biblical, theological, historical, and political facets of the conflict. In this second edition, Chapman offers clear analyses of Christian Zionism and its dispensationalist underpinnings.

Christison, Kathleen. *Perceptions of Palestine: Their Influence on US Middle East Policy.* Berkeley: University of California Press, 1999. Using insight gained during her work as a CIA analyst, Christison traces the contours of U.S. foreign policy through presidential administrations from Truman to Clinton.

Cramer, Richard Ben. *How Israel Lost: The Four Questions.* New York: Simon & Schuster, 2004. A former Middle East correspondent for the *Philadelphia Inquirer* and an American Jew, Cramer describes Palestinian life under occupation. He speculates that Israel's occupation is designed to "attack the grace and glue of Palestinian society, which is honor."

Drummond, Dorothy. *Holy Land, Whose Land? Modern Dilemma, Ancient Roots.* Seattle: Educare, 2002. A political geographer investigates the claims of many peoples (from "Abraham to Arafat") to the land called Holy.

El-Assal, Riah Abu. *Caught in Between: The Extraordinary Story of an Arab Palestinian Christian Israeli.* London: SPCK, 1999. Bishop Riah, Anglican leader in Jerusalem, tells the compelling story of one called to be a bridge builder.

Ellis, Marc H. *O Jerusalem! The Contested Future of the Jewish Covenant.* Minneapolis: Fortress Press, 1999. This American Jewish theologian examines God's covenant with the ancient Israelites in light of the oppression of Palestinians by the modern state of Israel. See also Ellis's *Israel and Palestine: Out of the Ashes* (London: Pluto, 2002); and *Toward a Jewish Theology of Liberation,* 3rd ed. (Waco, Tex.: Baylor University Press, 2004).

Farber, Seth. *Radicals, Rabbis and Peacemakers: Conversations with Jewish Critics of Israel* (Monroe, Maine: Common Courage Press, 2005). Farber, who edits and comments on these contributions from leading American Jewish critics of Israel's policies toward Palestinians, is a member of Jews Against the Occupation. Contributors include Phyllis Bennis, Noam Chomsky, Marc Ellis, Norman Finkelstein, Adam Shapiro, and seven others. Farber argues that Jews who support policies of Palestinian dispossession are jeopardizing Jews' relationship with God—the Covenant itself.

Forbes, Bruce D., and Jeanne H. Kilde, eds. *Rapture, Revelation, and the End Times: Exploring the Left Behind Series.* New York: Palgrave Macmillan, 2004. This collection of scholarly but accessible essays explores the various theological and political underpinnings of the Left Behind novels. The chapters written by Yaakov Ariel and Stanley Grenz are particularly helpful for mainline Christians seeking to understand the variety of evangelical perspectives on these matters.

Frykholm, Amy Johnson. *Rapture Culture: Left Behind in Evangelical America*. Oxford: Oxford University Press, 2004. An overview of the Left Behind novels and their theological, political, and cultural implications, including their impact on U.S. policy in the Middle East.

Gorenberg, Gershom. *End of Days: Fundamentalism and the Struggle for the Temple Mount*. New York: Free Press, 2000. The Temple Mount is the flash point of religious concern in the holy city of Jerusalem. Gorenberg, an Israeli journalist, focuses on the nexus of Jewish and Christian apocalyptic hopes and how, in Gorenberg's estimation, those shared visions result in troubling theological and political partnerships.

Hafften, Ann, ed. *Water from the Rock: Lutheran Voices from Palestine*. Minneapolis: Augsburg Fortress, 2003. Four Palestinian Lutherans and three U.S. Lutherans working in Palestine tell stories of health and hope seldom heard through the general media.

Hass, Amira. *Drinking the Sea at Gaza: Days and Nights in a Land under Siege*. New York: Henry Holt, 1996, 1999. An Israeli Jew, Hass went to Gaza as a human-rights volunteer, then became a reporter there for the Israeli daily *Ha'aretz*. She gives voice to Palestinians whose euphoria in the early days of the Oslo Accords yielded to despair and hopelessness.

Herzl, Theodor. *The Jewish State*, trans. Sylvie d'Avigdor. Mineola, N.Y.: Dover, 1988. A primary source document for secular Zionism, this slim book is essential to read if one is to understand the roots of Jewish concern regarding the need for a modern state. This edition is a reprint of a volume produced by the American Zionist Emergency Council (New York, 1946) to commemorate the fiftieth anniversary of the German-language original, *Der Judenstaat*.

Khalidi, Rashid. *Palestinian Identity: The Construction of Modern National Consciousness*. New York: Columbia University Press, 1998. Khalidi presents the most credible argument to date in English for the existence of an amorphous Palestinian territory with an identifiable population existing before the emergence of political Zionism.

Kimball, Charles. *When Religion Becomes Evil*. San Francisco: Harper, 2002. A post-9/11 look at five "danger signs" in religion: absolute truth claims, blind obedience, declaration of an "ideal time," insistence on the end justifying the means, and holy war.

Kimmerling, Baruch. *Politicide: Ariel Sharon's War against the Palestinians*. New York: Verso, 2003. An Israeli Jewish sociology professor writes that Prime Minister Sharon's ultimate goal is "dissolution of the Palestinian people's existence as a legitimate social, political and economic entity."

Kushner, Tony, and Alisa Solomon, eds. *Wrestling with Zion: Progressive Jewish-American Responses to the Israeli-Palestinian Conflict.* New York: Grove, 2003. This collection of writings from a large number of American Jews documents the varieties of dissent voiced within this diverse community.

Lerner, Michael. *The Geneva Accord and Other Strategies for Healing the Israeli-Palestinian Conflict.* Berkeley, Calif.: North Atlantic Books, 2004. A basically positive treatment of the unofficial agreement issued by a group of Palestinian and Israeli figures in December 2003. Lerner, a rabbi, has also authored *Healing Israel/Palestine* (Berkeley, Calif.: North Atlantic Books, 2003).

Morris, Benny. *Righteous Victims: A History of the Zionist-Arab Conflict.* New York: Vintage, 2001. From the beginnings of the modern Zionist movement, Morris traces the social and cultural history of the relationship between Palestinian Arabs and Israeli Jews.

Nassar, Alison Jones, with Fred Strickert. *Imm Mathilda: A Bethlehem Mother's Diary.* Minneapolis: Kirk House, 2003. An American living with her Palestinian Lutheran husband and three young daughters in occupied Bethlehem writes about the daily struggle to maintain hope. Strickert is a religion professor at Wartburg College, Waverly, Iowa.

Prior, Michael, ed. *Speaking the Truth about Zionism and Israel.* London: Melisende, 2004. Archbishop Desmond Tutu says in his foreword, "The distinguished contributors from Israel, Palestine, the US, the UK, and Ireland, women and men, Jews, Christians, and Muslims speak their truth. Reconciliation will come later."

Qumsiyeh, Mazin B. *Sharing the Land of Canaan: Human Rights and the Israeli-Palestinian Struggle.* London: Pluto, 2004. A Palestinian makes the argument that Canaan, a name based on an ancient shared history, must inevitably be shared by Israelis and Palestinians. He bases his case in human rights and international law, economics and environmental practicalities.

Raheb, Mitri. *Bethlehem Besieged: Stories of Hope in Times of Trouble.* Minneapolis: Fortress Press, 2004. The pastor of Evangelical Lutheran Christmas Church in Bethlehem shares the effort of Holy Land Christians to give hope to people living under military occupation. See also Raheb's *I Am a Palestinian Christian* (Minneapolis: Fortress Press, 1995).

Ross, Dennis. *The Missing Peace: The Inside Story of the Fight for Middle East Peace.* New York: Farrar, Straus & Giroux, 2004. The history of failed Arab-Israeli peace negotiations from 1991 to 2001 is told by the U.S. diplomat who was centrally involved, under both Republican and Democratic administrations. Ross argues that while an eventual peace is inevitable, it will not come until there is aggressive participation by a U.S. president.

Rossing, Barbara R. *The Rapture Exposed: The Message of Hope in the Book of Revelation*. Boulder, Colo.: Westview, 2004. A New Testament scholar, Rossing portrays the Rapture ideology as a specific threat to the fragile peace process in the Holy Land. She sees the dispensationalist theology, exemplified by the Left Behind novels, as biblical fiction and Christian heresy.

Ruether, Rosemary Radford, and Herman J. Ruether. *The Wrath of Jonah: The Crisis of Religious Nationalism in the Israeli-Palestinian Conflict*. Minneapolis: Fortress Press, 2002. A theological-political analysis of the convergence of nationalisms and fundamentalisms.

Said, Edward. *Culture and Resistance*. Cambridge, Mass.: South End Press, 2003. Perhaps this era's most prominent Palestinian-American scholar and intellectual shares his thoughts on terrorism and the Israel-Palestine conflict, and provides a vision for a secular, democratic future in the Middle East. See also *Covering Islam: How the Media and the Experts Determine How We See the Rest of the World*, rev. ed. (New York: Vintage, 1997); *Peace and Its Discontents: Essays on Palestine in the Middle East Peace Process* (New York: Vintage, 1996); and *The Question of Palestine*, 2nd ed. (New York: Vintage, 1992).

Sennott, Charles M. *The Body and the Blood: The Holy Land's Christians at the Turn of a New Millennium*. New York: Public Affairs/Perseus, 2001. A look at the "ongoing agony in the gardens of Israel and Palestine." Explores the unique role given to the Christian minority as a necessary bridge between Jews and Muslims.

Sizer, Stephen. *Christian Zionism: Road-Map to Armageddon?* (Leicester, U.K.: InterVarsity Press, 2004). Don Wagner, of North Park University in Chicago, says, "Sizer's work is the most important and comprehensive on the subject to date. [He] raises vital theological and political challenges that must be addressed head-on by Christians in the West, particularly evangelicals."

Stern, Jessica. *Terror in the Name of God: Why Religious Militants Kill*. New York: Harper Perennial, 2002. The result of a four-year exploration into the thinking of religious terrorists—Christian, Jewish, and Muslim. Holy Land extremists figure large in Stern's report, though she talks with individuals from Florida to Pakistan.

Swisher, Clayton E. *The Truth about Camp David: The Untold Story about the Collapse of the Middle East Peace Process*. New York: Nation, 2004. Swisher's work, based on detailed interviews with dozens of high-level American and Middle East participants, challenges the myth that Israel made a "generous offer" to the Palestinians at Camp David in 2000. Swisher, a former Marine reservist and federal criminal investigator, offers an alternative to the perspective of Dennis Ross in *The Missing Peace*.

Thomas, Baylis. *How Israel Was Won: A Concise History of the Arab-Israel Conflict*. Lexington, Mass.: Lexington Books, 1999. A balanced treatment of the Israeli state's conception, creation, and expansion, from the 1896 birth of Zionism to the death of the Oslo Accords a century later. Especially useful are Thomas's treatments of the initial expansionist goals of Israel's founders, the way Jewish nationalism emerges uniquely from the Holocaust, and the difficulty of claiming to be a democracy while not granting full rights to non-Jewish citizens.

Wagner, Donald E. *Dying in the Land of Promise: Palestine and Palestinian Christianity from Pentecost to 2000*, 2nd ed. London: Melisende, 2003. A look at the endangered future faced by Christians in the "land of promise." Wagner envisions that, with a just resolution of the conflict, Palestinian Christians will play a key role in building bridges of reconciliation. See also *Anxious for Armageddon: A Call to Partnership for Middle Eastern and Western Christians* (Scottdale, Pa.: Herald, 1995).

Younan, Munib. *Witnessing for Peace: In Jerusalem and the World*. Minneapolis: Fortress Press, 2003. The Lutheran bishop of Jerusalem shares the story of Arab Christianity in the Holy Land, his own theology of nonviolence, and his commitment to Palestinian rights and to reconciliation with Israelis.

Zunes, Stephen. *Tinderbox: U.S. Middle East Policy and the Roots of Terrorism*. Monroe, Maine: Common Courage Press, 2003. Explains "why they hate us"—how U.S. foreign policy over many decades has led to disgust and hostility throughout the Arab and Muslim world.

Videos

Beyond the Mirage: The Face of the Occupation. DVD, 47 min. Santa Barbara, Calif.: Americans for a Just Peace in the Middle East, 2002. Israeli and Palestinian voices discuss violations of human rights resulting from Israel's military occupation of Palestinian territory, the longest in modern history. Featured is Jeff Halper, an American Jew who is now director of the Israeli Committee Against House Demolitions. Available for purchase from Americans for Middle East Understanding, www.ameu.org, or call 212.870.2053.

The Dividing Wall. DVD and VHS, 23 min. Akron, Pa.: Mennonite Central Committee, 2004. Exploring the humanitarian, social, and political impact of the Israeli-built "security barrier," this video comes with study guide and advocacy suggestions. Order from Mennonite Central Committee, Box 500, Akron, PA 17501-0500; visit www.thenovgroup.com/MCC/catalog/, or telephone, toll-free, 888.563.4676.

Dreams of Justice and Freedom with Hanan Ashrawi. DVD and VHS, 52 min. Directed by Christopher Swann. 1995. The Palestinian human-rights activist tackles the issues at the heart of her people's struggle for a homeland. With compassion and eloquence, Ashrawi calls for an end to the occupation on humanitarian rather than ideological grounds. Available from Arab Film Distribution at www.arabfilm.com.

"Healing in a Holy Land," *Mosaic.* VHS, 20 min. Chicago: Evangelical Lutheran Church in America, autumn 1999. Other segments of this video magazine are titled "Dreams of the Future" and "Christians of the Pentecost." Order from the ELCA Dept. for Communication, www.elca.org/mosaic, or call 800.638.3522, ext. 6009.

Peace, Propaganda, and the Promised Land. DVD and VHS, 80 min. Northampton, Mass.: Media Education Foundation, 2004. Exposes how foreign-policy interests of U.S. political elites, working in combination with Israeli public relations strategies, exercise powerful influence on news reporting of the Middle East conflict. Features U.S. and British TV news clips with observations of analysts, journalists, and activists. Order from the Media Education Foundation, www.mediaed.org, or call 800.897.0089.

Peacemaking in the Holy Land: A Sacred Call. VHS, 20 min. New York: Episcopal Church, 1999. Created for the Episcopal Church in the United States, this video explores the conflict through the lens of Christian peace seekers. Order from Episcopal Parish Services, www.episcopalparishservices.org, or call 800.638.5544.

Salt of the Earth: Palestinian Christians in the Northern West Bank. DVD, 135 min. Louisville: Salt Films, n.d. Produced by Presbyterian Church (U.S.A.) missionaries, this video is divided into nine chapters that address various issues of concern for Christians living in the West Bank. Topics covered include the separation wall, freedom of movement, refugee issues, education, security, and Christian Zionism. The film's Web site includes a study guide written by the producers. Available from Salt Films at www.saltfilms.net.

Tragedy in the Holy Land: The Second Uprising. DVD and VHS, 71 min. Directed by Denis Mueler. 2002. Addresses the core issues of land and identity, using rarely seen archival footage and interviews with scholarly experts. Probes the conflict from a historical perspective typically unknown to American audiences. Available from Arab Film Distribution at www.arabfilm.com.

Web Sites

General Edcucation/Advocacy Sites

American-Arab Anti-Discrimination Committee. Founded in 1980 by Senator James Abourezk of South Dakota, ADC is committed to "defending the civil rights of all people of Arab heritage in the United States" and "encouraging a balanced U.S. foreign policy in the Middle East. www.adc.org

American Israel Public Affairs Committee. "America's Pro-Israel Lobby," the influential voice with Congress and the White House in support of Israeli government activity. www.aipac.org

Americans for Middle East Understanding. AMEU strives to create in the United States a deeper appreciation of the culture, history, and current events in the Middle East; it publishes a bimonthly, "The Link." www.ameu.org

Amnesty International. A movement of people who campaign for internationally recognized human rights, including those of persons in Israel and the occupied territories. www.amnesty.org

Applied Research Institute. A nonprofit organization dedicated to promoting sustainable development in the Palestinian occupied territories. www.arij.org

B'tselem, the Israeli Information Center for Human Rights in the Occupied Territories. Documents rights violations by Israel's government and results of terrorist attacks by Palestinians and Israelis. www.btselem.org

Coalition of Women for Peace. A group of Israeli agencies representing concerned women, including Bat Shalom and the Women in Black. www.coalitionofwomen.org

Electronic Intifada. A nongovernmental effort committed to "comprehensive public education on the question of Palestine, the Israeli-Palestinian conflict, and the economic, political, legal, and human dimensions of Israel's 38-year occupation of Palestinian territories." www.electronicintifada.net

Foundation for Middle East Peace. "A non-profit organization dedicated to informing Americans about the Israeli-Palestinian conflict and assisting in a peaceful solution that brings security for both peoples." Publishes the Report on Israeli Settlement in the Occupied Territories. www.fmep.org

Gush Shalom. The name of this Israeli group is Hebrew for "Peace Bloc." It provides a list of products produced in Israeli settlements on Palestinian territory and encourages international consumer boycott of the same. www.gush-shalom.org

Human Rights Watch. "Dedicated to protecting the human rights of people around the world." Click on "Middle East/N. Africa." www.hrw.org

If Americans Knew. Seeks to provide Americans with facts to inform their citizenship behavior, especially on the Israel / Palestine situation. www.ifamericansknew.org

International Solidarity Movement. "A Palestinian-led movement committed to resisting the Israeli occupation of Palestinian land, using nonviolent, direct-action methods and principles." www.palsolidarity.org

Israeli Committee against House Demolitions. Group of Israeli citizens who stand with Palestinians whose homes are threatened with destruction by Israel's government. www.icahd.org

Israeli Council for Israeli-Palestinian Peace. Publishes a newsletter, "The Other Israel," devoted to pursuit of a just peace. http://otherisrael.home.igc.org

Jewish Voice for Peace. "Represents the silent majority of American Jews who want an end to the occupation and settlements, and who want to see a U.S. foreign policy based on justice." www.jewishvoiceforpeace.org

Jews for Justice in the Middle East. Publishes analyses that seek to be balanced, including "The Origin of the Palestine-Israel Conflict." www.cactus48.com/truth.html

Middle East Children's Alliance. "A non-profit organization working for justice in the Middle East focusing on the Occupied Palestinian Territories, Israel, and Occupied Iraq." www.mecaforpeace.org

Palestine Monitor. Palestinian Non-Governmental Network's effort to do education and advocacy on behalf of Palestinians with the world community. www.palestinemonitor.org

Palestinian Centre for Rapprochement Between People. A Palestinian program that seeks peace and reconciliation with Israelis. www.rapprochement.org

Palestinian Environmental NGOs. A nonprofit agency coordinating opposition to land and water confiscation by Israeli settlements in the occupied territories. www.pengon.org

Palestinian Initiative for the Promotion of Global Dialogue and Democracy. A nongovernmental group headed by the Palestinian educator Dr. Hanan Ashrawi. www.miftah.org

Rabbis for Human Rights. Group of Israeli Jewish rabbis who take direct action to defend human rights of Palestinians. www.rhr.israel.net

Search for Justice and Equality in Palestine/Israel. Led by Ned Hanauer, an American Jewish political scientist, Search for Justice focuses on media advocacy. www.searchforjustice.org

Somerville Divestment Project. A grassroots campaign asking Somerville, Massachusetts, to remove city retirement funds from Israel bonds and U.S. companies that supply military arms to Israel. Good source of updates on the divestment movement in general. www.divestmentproject.org

Tikkun Community. "An international community of people of many faiths calling for social justice and political freedom," led by a U.S. Jewish rabbi, Michael Lerner. Publishes *Tikkun*, a bimonthly magazine. Palestine-Israel peace is a top priority for Tikkun (Hebrew for "to heal, repair, transform the world"). www.tikkun.org

Trans-Arab Research Institute. A U.S.-based academic effort that "aims to provide focused research and public venues to analyze, discuss, and present optional perspectives" on destabilizing Middle East concerns. www. tari.org

United Nations Division of Palestinian Rights. Information on the history of the Palestine-Israel conflict, UN actions and programs, plus current assessments and maps. www.un.org/depts/dpa/qpal

United Nations Office for Coordination of Humanitarian Affairs, Occupied Palestinian Territory. "Working to end the humanitarian crisis in the occupied Palestinian territory." www.ochaopt.org

United Nations Relief and Works Agency (UNWRA). This organization, since creation of the state of Israel, has been responsible for providing humanitarian support to Palestinian refugees. www.un.org/unwra

United States Embassy, Tel Aviv, Israel. Source of current U.S. government stances on Israel-Palestine situation, latest travel advice for the region, and human-rights reports for Israel and occupied territories. www. usembassy-israel.org.il

Unity Coalition for Israel. A stridently pro-Israel-government (except on Gaza withdrawal) agency that brings together Jewish and Christian groups. Strong opposition to the road map. "Israel is not just a Jewish issue. Millions of Christians resolutely endorse the principle of peace with security for the state of Israel." www.israelunitycoalition.org

U.S. Campaign to End the Occupation. "We aim to change those U.S. policies that sustain Israel's 38-year occupation of the Palestinian West Bank,
Gaza, and East Jerusalem. . . . such as the billions of U.S. military and
economic aid dollars provided despite Israel's violations of U.S. and international law." www.endtheoccupation.org

Washington Report on Middle East Affairs. A magazine published by the American Educational Trust, a nonprofit foundation organized by retired U.S.
foreign service officers "to provide the American public with balanced
and accurate information concerning U.S. relations with Middle Eastern
states." www.wrmea.org

Wheels of Justice. "Nonviolent education and action against war and occupation in Iraq and Palestine for justice and universal human rights." Con-
ducts tours around North America. www.justicewheels.org

Sites Related to Church Agencies

American Friends Service Committee. Seeks to implement "Quaker values
in action." Click on "Israel-Palestine Peacebuilding Program." www.afsc.
org/middleeast/default.htm

Bethlehem Media Center. A program of Christmas Lutheran Church's International Center which seeks to tell Palestinian stories not covered by
the general media. Click on "Media and Communication Center." www.
annadwa.org

Bridges for Peace. A group with Christian Zionist orientation, self-described
as "a Jerusalem-based, Bible-believing Christian organization supporting Israel and building relationships between Christians and Jews worldwide." www.bridgesforpeace.org

Challenging Christian Zionism: Christians Committed to Biblical Justice. A
campaign organized by evangelical Christians in opposition to the theology and politics of Christian Zionists. www.christianzionism.org

Christian Peacemaker Teams. This ministry of the U.S. historic peace churches
has a team working in Hebron, occupied West Bank. www.cpt.org

Churches for Middle East Peace. An ecumenical working group of twenty-one
Orthodox, Protestant, and Roman Catholic policy offices in Washington,
D.C. www.cmep.org

Ecumenical Accompaniment Programme in Palestine and Israel. Provides
on-site accompaniers with Palestinian and Israeli peace/human-rights
groups. Organized by World Council of Churches in consultation with
Holy Land churches. www.eappi.org

Episcopal Peace Fellowship. An independent group working within the U.S. Episcopal Church. Enter "Episcopal Church and Israel" in SEARCH. www.episcopalpeacefellowship.org

Evangelical Lutheran Church in America, Division of Global Ministry. Largest U.S. Lutheran body has campaign, "Peace Not Walls," seeking justice and peace in the Holy Land. www.elca.org/middleeast

Evangelical Lutheran Church in Jordan and the Holy Land. A Palestinian denomination with six congregations, five schools, and other service agencies in the West Bank, Jerusalem, and Jordan. www.holyland-lutherans.org

Evangelicals for Middle East Understanding. "An affiliation of North American Christian churches, agencies, and individuals which seeks to provide encouragement to, advocacy for, and fellowship with Christians in the Middle East." www.emeu.net

Holy Land Christian Ecumenical Foundation. An organization seeking "to educate Western Christians about the urgent needs of Christians in the Holy Land." www.hcef.org

Lutheran World Federation, Department of World Service. This agency of the Lutheran world community operates health and educational ministries serving Palestinians. www.lwfjerusalem.org

Mennonite Church USA. Click on "Peace Resources" and enter "Palestine/Israel." www.mennonitechurcheusa.org

Middle East Council of Churches. This organization brings together, for work in unity and social service, churches from four traditions: Eastern Orthodox, Oriental Orthodox, Protestant, and Roman Catholic. It has offices in Jerusalem, plus Cyprus, Egypt, Jordan, and United Arab Emirates. www.mec-churches.org

National Interreligious Initiative for Peace in the Middle East. Thirty-three leaders of U.S. Christian, Jewish, and Muslim bodies seeking to influence U.S. government involvement with resolution of the Israel-Palestine conflict. www.walktheroadtopeace.org

Pax Christi USA. A Roman Catholic peace movement. Click on "Coordinated Awareness Raising Campaign on Israel-Palestine." www.paxchristi.net

Peaceful Ends through Peaceful Means. An initiative of Churches for Middle East Peace, Church World Service, and the National Council of Churches, in support of Israelis and Palestinians who work for peace. www.pepm.org

Presbyterian Church U.S.A. Click on "U.S. and World Mission," then "Presbyterians at work around the world," then "Middle East." Includes "Guidelines for Implementation of Phased, Selective Divestment. www.pcusa.org

Sabeel International. "An ecumenical grassroots liberation movement among Palestinian Christians [working] to promote a more accurate international awareness regarding the identity, presence, and witness of Palestinian Christians. www.sabeel.org. See also Friends of Sabeel North America. www.fosna.org

United Church of Christ, Office for Middle East and Europe. Includes recent actions on "Use of Economic Leverage in Promoting Peace in the Middle East." gmtest.ucc.org/mee

United Methodist Church, General Board of Church and Society. Click on "World Community," then "Middle East" under Issues. www.umc-gbcs.org

The village of Jayyous is cut off by the separation wall from much of its access to farmland and water wells. The ground had been razed by Israeli bulldozers. In protest, this young boy was chosen by village leaders to carry a young olive tree to be replanted in the path of the oncoming wall. The wall now covers this land.

Notes

Chapter 1. What's So Special about This Space?

1. "The Jerusalem Sabeel Document" of 2004, issued by the Palestinian Christian liberation theology center in Jerusalem, underscores this point. It says, "The land of Palestine/Israel, as the whole world, belongs to God. We are all tenants and aliens on it. God has placed us Palestinians and Israelis on the land. We must share it and be good stewards of it (Psalm 24:1, Lev. 25:23, Ezek. 47:21-23)." For a readable book-length survey of the geographic, ethnic, religious, and political elements in claims to this land over four thousand years, see Dorothy Drummond, *Holy Land, Whose Land? Modern Dilemma, Ancient Roots* (Seattle: Educare Press, 2002).

2. Exact membership figures are impossible to find, but rough estimates (gathered from Bailey and Bailey, *Who Are the Christians in the Middle East?*) suggest these totals for Christian groups in the Holy Land:

	Israel Proper	Occupied Territories	Total
Greek Orthodox	35,000	40,000	75,000
Latin Catholic (Maronite, Melkite, Latin-Rite, other)	54,000	19,000	73,000
Oriental Orthodox (Armenian, Syrian, Coptic, Ethiopian)	2,000	8,000	10,000
Evangelical (Protestant)			
Anglican	1,100	2,500	3,600
Lutheran	—	2,400	2,400
Other	1,500	500	2,000
	93,600	**72,400**	**166,000**

3. William Dalrymple, "Disappearing Christians," *New York Review of Books*, September 25, 2003.

4. Charles M. Sennott, *The Body and the Blood: The Holy Land's Christians at the Turn of a New Millennium* (New York: Public Affairs, 2001), xix. An organization working "to educate Western Christians about the urgent needs of Christians in Palestine and Israel" is the Holy Land Christian Ecumenical Foundation, 6935 Wisconsin Ave., #214, Bethesda, MD 20815; Web site: www.hcef.org.

5. George Hintlian, "Reflections of a Jerusalem Christian," *Bitterlemons International* 2(43) (December 9, 2004), www.bitterlemons-international.org.

6. Naim S. Ateek, "Biblical Perspectives on the Land," in *Faith and the Intifada: Palestinian Christian Voices*, ed. Naim S. Ateek, Marc H. Ellis, and Rosemary Radford Ruether (Maryknoll, N.Y.: Orbis, 1992), 114.

7. Donald Bridge, *Travelling through the Promised Land* (Ross-shire, U.K.: Christian Focus, 1998), 14–15.

8. These "facts on the ground" have led some Israelis and some Palestinians to argue for a one-state resolution of the conflict, in which all the ten-million-plus inhabitants of the land come together in a single, secular, democratic state with equal rights for all. But majorities of both Israelis and Palestinians see a one-state solution as impossible.

9. Mark Zeitoun, "Avoiding a Mideast Water War," *Washington Post*, February 4, 2004, A23. Zeitoun is a humanitarian-aid water engineer who has worked in several Middle East settings.

10. Bernard Avishai, *The Tragedy of Zionism: Revolution and Democracy in the Land of Israel* (New York: Helios, 1985), 244, quoted in Karen Armstrong, *Holy War: The Crusades and Their Impact on Today's World*, 2nd ed. (New York: Anchor, 2001), 283–84.

11. Keep in mind that most such criticisms come from Christians in mainline church traditions; so-called Christian Zionists are notoriously uncritical of Israeli government policies. This sad division within the same faith family is mostly a phenomenon among Christians in the United States. A superb treatment of how "Rapture theology" connects with Christian Zionism and right-wing politics in Israel is Barbara Rossing, *The Rapture Exposed: The Message of Hope in the Book of Revelation* (Boulder, Colo.: Westview, 2004).

12. Natan Sharansky, "Antisemitism in 3-D," *Forward*, January 21, 2005, www.forward.com.

13. People called Arabs are not what one would consider newcomers to this land. They were present on Pentecost Day for the birth of the church (Acts 2:11). Moreover, Arabs (and thus many Muslims) trace their heritage to Abraham's first son, Ishmael, to whom God made promises alongside the covenant established through Isaac (Gen 17:20).

14. Dietrich Bonhoeffer, *Letters and Papers from Prison*, enlarged ed., ed. Eberhard Bethge (New York: Macmillan, 1972), 370.

15. The call was issued by Michel Sabbah, Latin Patriarch of Jerusalem; Riah Abu El-Assal, Bishop of Jerusalem, Episcopal Church of Jerusalem and the Middle East; and Munib Younan, Bishop of Jerusalem, Evangelical Lutheran Church in Jordan and the Holy Land. Their message concluded with quotation of 1 Cor 12:26, "If one member suffers, all suffer together with it; if one member is honored, all rejoice together with it."

Chapter 2. Politics, Faiths, and Fundamentalisms

1. The name of the church over which Bishop Younan presides can be a bit confusing. When it was first recognized in 1959 by Jordan's King Hussein, all of the denomination's six congregations were in Jordanian territory. Thus, for many years, the church was the ELCJ, the Evangelical Lutheran Church in Jordan. With the 1967 war and Israel's subsequent occupation of the West Bank, five of those congregations found themselves in what the UN then recognized as occupied Palestinian territory. It has recently added "and the Holy Land" to its name.

2. The complex nature of this conversation is underscored by the fact that naming the land sitting at the heart of the conflict discussed here is itself a political act. In this chapter, "Israel/Palestine" will refer to the general geographic area while "state of Israel" and "occupied Palestinian territories" will serve to demarcate the pre-1967 border areas.

3. Walter Brueggemann, *The Land: Place as Gift, Promise, and Challenge in Biblical Faith*, 2nd ed. (Minneapolis: Fortress Press, 2002), 202. Brueggemann continues, "And unless we address the land question with Jews, we shall not likely understand the locus of meaning or the issue of identity. The Jewish community—in all its long, tortuous history—has never forgotten that its roots and its hopes are in storied earth, and that is the central driving force of its uncompromising ethical faith."

4. George Robinson, *Essential Judaism: A Complete Guide to Beliefs, Customs and Rituals* (New York: Pocket Books, 2000), 261. For a more detailed discussion of the following biblical traditions, see the second part of Gary Burge, *Whose Land? Whose Promise? What Christians Are Not Being Told about Israel and the Palestinians* (Cleveland: Pilgrim, 2003).

5. Jews typically engage the Hebrew Bible in a manner quite distinct from typical Christian approaches to Scripture. To put the difference simplistically, while Christian discourse often assumes Scripture as its starting point, Jewish discourse is generally shaped first by present concerns, which are then informed by the textual tradition. Even religious Jews are unlikely to reference Scripture to support a point they are trying to make, at least not with the same "prooftexting" method common in many Christian circles. Biblical traditions surrounding the land, therefore, are not the final word for most Jewish communities. Still, while most Jews today, even those living within the state of Israel, would not appeal first to biblical writings to

justify the modern Jewish state, those traditions have been crucial in garnering the support of other communities (especially Western Christians).

6. The conditionality of the covenant is most pronounced in Deuteronomy, giving rise to what has been termed the "Deuteronomistic" theological perspective.

7. *Mishna Torah*, Kings 6:10, cited in David L. Lieber et al., eds., *Etz Hayim: Torah and Commentary* (Philadelphia: Jewish Publication Society, 2001), 1104. This perspective was shared with me by Rabbi Paula Reimers when I showed her pictures of Palestinian olive groves uprooted in November 2002 to make way for Israel's separation barrier.

8. The following historical discussion draws heavily from Colin Chapman, "Is 'Jerusalem' a Christian Cause?" *Theological Review* 24(2) (2003): 98–126.

9. Most importantly, the Temple was the dwelling place of God's *Shekinah*. Derived from the Hebrew "to dwell" (*shakan*), *Shekinah* came to be accepted as a description or name for the God of Israel.

10. Chapman, "Jerusalem," 102.

11. See the discussion of Rabbi Irving Greenberg's concept of Jewish history in Marc H. Ellis, *Toward a Jewish Theology of Liberation: The Challenge of the 21st Century* (Waco, Tex.: Baylor University Press, 2004).

12. The day has historical significance for many other terrible events in Jewish history. See Robinson, *Essential Judaism*, 131–33.

13. Ibid., 122. In Jerusalem, Jews state, "Next year in a Jerusalem rebuilt."

14. W. D. Davies, *The Gospel and the Land: Early Christianity and Jewish Territorial Doctrine* (Berkeley: University of California Press, 1974), 375, 179, quoted in Colin Chapman, *Whose Promised Land? The Continuing Crisis over Israel and Palestine* (Grand Rapids: Baker, 2002), 141.

15. Franklin Littell, *The Crucifixion of the Jews* (New York: Harper & Row, 1975), 2.

16. See, for instance, Midge Decter, "A Jew in Anti-Christian America," *First Things*, October 1995, 25–31.

17. Chapman, "Jerusalem," 98.

18. Matthew 24:1-2; Mark 13:1-2; Luke 21:5-6. Even with the destruction of the Temple, the Abrahamic covenant is an important foundation for the New Testament. See, for instance, Mary's Magnificat: "[The LORD] has helped his servant Israel, in remembrance of his mercy, according to the promise he made to our ancestors, to Abraham and to his descendants forever" (Luke 1:54-55).

19. Chapman, "Jerusalem," 121.

20. Karen Armstrong, *Jerusalem: One City, Three Faiths* (New York: Knopf, 1996), 274.

21. Charles M. Sennott, *The Body and the Blood: The Holy Land's Christians at the Turn of a New Millennium, A Reporter's Journey* (New York: Public Affairs/ Perseus, 2001), 87.

22. Armstrong, *Jerusalem*, 370.

23. All Qur'anic references are from Muhammad Taqī-ud-Dīn Al-Hilālī and Muhammad Muhsin Khān, *Translation of the Meanings of The Noble Qur'an in the English Language* (Medina, Saudi Arabia: King Fahd Complex, n.d.).

24. While the concept discussed here is technically supersessionist, traditional Islamic perspectives do not naturally harbor the same anti-Semitic "eliminationist" supersessionism contained in some Christian theological perspectives (see Littell, *The Crucifixion of the Jews*).

25. Chapman, "Jerusalem," 112.

26. The Arabic word *islam*, translated "submission," does not necessarily evoke the entire religious system known by that name.

27. Mohammed Abdul Hameed Al-Khateeb, *Al-Quds: The Place of Jerusalem in Classical Judaic and Islamic Traditions* (London: Ta-Ha, 1998), 131, cited in Chapman, *Whose Promised Land?* 267.

28. Armstrong, *Jerusalem*, 294.

29. Peter L. Berger, "Reflections on the Sociology of Religion Today: The 2000 Paul Hanly Furfey Lecture," *Sociology of Religion* 62(4) (2001), 445.

30. For an analysis of the internal struggles of both Zionism and Palestinian nationalism following the Gaza disengagement, see Steven Erlanger, "Gaza Pullout Displays New Scars for Palestinians and Israelis," *New York Times*, August 22, 2005.

31. Nur Masalha, "A Critique on Benny Morris," in *The Israel/Palestine Question*, ed. Ilan Pappe (New York: Routledge, 1999), 218.

32. Cited in ibid., 215.

33. *Fateh*, literally meaning "victory" or "conquest," is also a reverse acronym of *Harakat al-Tahrir al-Watani al-Filastini*, Palestinian National Liberation Movement. *Hamas*, Arabic for "zeal," is an acronym for *Harakat al muqāwama al-Islamiyya*, Islamic Resistance Movement. An "Islamist" is someone who understands Islam as a system that should influence all spheres of life. Care should be taken to not confuse Islamism with mere militancy or extremism.

34. Khaled Hroub, *Hamas: Political Thought and Practice* (Washington, D.C.: Institute for Palestine Studies, 2000), 39.

35. "Hamas Platform," in ibid., 274.

36. Andrea Nüsse, *Muslim Palestine: The Ideology of Hamas* (Amsterdam: Harwood, 1998), 49.

37. Ilan Pappe, ed., *The Israel/Palestine Question* (New York: Routledge, 1999), 3.

38. Kathleen Christison, *Perceptions of Palestine: Their Influence on US Middle East Policy* (Berkeley: University of California Press, 1999).

39. Edward W. Said, *The Question of Palestine*, 2nd ed. (New York: Vintage, 1992), xl.

40. "Hamas was committed to attacking only 'legitimate military targets,' and in the early years up to 1994 it did not target civilians. The movement declared this commitment more than once and did not violate it except in the seventh year of its existence, and only after the Hebron massacre and in accordance with the principle of reciprocity" (Hroub, *Hamas*, 245–46). The "Hebron massacre" refers to American-born Kiryat Arba resident Baruch Goldstein's February 25, 1994, slaughter of twenty-nine Palestinians as they knelt in prayer at the Mosque of the Tomb of Abraham in Hebron, during the month of Ramadan. The integrity of this commitment not to target civilians has been acknowledged by Israeli analysts. See Ehud Sprinzak, "How Israel Misjudges Hamas and Its Terrorism," *Washington Post*, October 19, 1997. From the perspective of Hamas, Israeli settlers do not have the same "civilian" status as Israelis within the 1967 borders.

41. Mahmoud Abbas, *Istithmar al-fawaz* [Utilizing the victory] (Kuwait: Union of Palestinian Writers and Journalists, 1983), quoted in Hroub, *Hamas*, 248.

42. Jessica Stern, *Terror in the Name of God: Why Religious Militants Kill* (New York: Ecco, 2003), 105–6.

43. Quoted in Stephen Zunes, *Tinderbox: US Foreign Policy and the Roots of Terrorism* (Monroe, Maine: Common Courage, 2003), 129.

44. Gershom Gorenberg, *End of Days: Fundamentalism and the Struggle for the Temple Mount* (New York: Free Press, 2000), 136.

45. Martin Gilbert, *Israel: A History* (New York: Doubleday, 1998), 566, quoted in Chapman, *Whose Promised Land?* 241.

46. Fears of what happened to Rabin and the peace process in which he engaged inspired a spirited editorial from Jeffrey Goldberg, "Protect Sharon from the Right," *New York Times*, August 5, 2004. Zeev Sternhell locates this resistance in the marrow of political Zionism itself: "Peace is a mortal danger to the Zionism of blood and soil, a Zionism that cannot imagine willingly returning even one inch of the sacred territory of the land of Israel." In *The Founding Myths of Israel: Nationalism, Socialism, and the Making of the Jewish State*, trans. David Maisel (Princeton: Princeton University Press, 1998), 343.

47. From fiscal year 1949 to fiscal year 2003, the United States has provided Israel with military aid, grants, and loan guarantees totaling over $90 billion. Clyde R. Mark, "Israel: US Foreign Assistance," Library of Congress Congressional Research Service Brief for Congress (updated May 14, 2003). As of 2005, the amount is right at $100 billion.

48. Brueggemann, *The Land*, 203.

49. A good introduction to Middle Eastern Christianity, including Palestinian communities, can be found in Betty Jane Bailey and J. Martin Bailey, *Who Are the Christians in the Middle East?* (Grand Rapids: Eerdmans, 2003).

50. Elias Chacour with Mary E. Jensen, *We Belong to the Land: The Story of a Palestinian Israeli Who Lives for Peace and Reconciliation*, 2nd ed. (Notre Dame, Ind.: University of Notre Dame Press, 2001), 113.

Chapter 3. Division in the Christian Family

1. The full name of the peace plan, endorsed also by the European Community, Russia, and the United Nations, is "A Performance-Based Roadmap to a Permanent Two-State Solution to the Israeli-Palestinian Conflict."

2. As stated by Senator Rudy Boschwitz (R.-Minn.), Chairman of the Senate Foreign Relations Committee's Subcommittee on the Middle East (December 12, 1982). Cited in Nimrod Novik, *The United States and Israel: Domestic Determinants of a Changing US Commitment* (Boulder, Colo.: Westview, 1986), 71.

3. See Steven T. Rosenthal, *Irreconcilable Differences? The Waning of the American Jewish Love Affair with Israel* (Hanover, N.J.: Brandeis University Press, 2001).

4. Novik, *The United States and Israel*, 71.

5. Daphna Berman, "Robertson: If Bush 'Touches' Jerusalem, We'll Form 3rd Party," *Ha'aretz*, October 4, 2004. A year later it was reported that the Israeli government will lease, to a group of U.S. Evangelicals led by Pat Robertson, 125 acres of land on Lake Kinneret (Sea of Galilee) between Capernaum and Tabgha for construction of a Christian-oriented visitor center and biblical theme park—"Israel to lease Kinneret shore land to Evangelicals," Irit Rosenblum, *Ha'aretz*, October 10, 2005.

6. Donald Wagner, "Reagan and Begin, Bibi and Jerry: The Theopolitical Alliance of the Likud Party with the American Christian 'Right,'" *Arab Studies Quarterly* 20(4) (fall 1998): 34.

7. L. Nelson Bell, "Unfolding Destiny," *Christianity Today* 11(21) (July 21, 1967): 28. An editorial one month earlier carried this title: "War Sweeps the Bible Lands: Frantic Nations Forget That the Prophetic Vision of World Peace Is Messianic," *Christianity Today* 9(19) (June 23, 1967). There, it was noted that UN concerns are marginal relative to God's prophetic timetable.

8. Ronald R. Stockton, "Christian Zionism: Prophecy and Public Opinion," *Middle East Journal* 41(2) (spring 1987): 234–54.

9. Pew Forum on Religion and Public Life, "American Evangelicals and Israel," Fact Sheet, http://pewforum.org.

10. Brent Boyer, "Arvada Church Champions Jewish Cause: Christian Zionists Back Jewish People," *Denver Post*, November 22, 2002; and Lou Gonzales, "Marketing Team Reaches Out to Christian Zionists," *Colorado Springs Gazette*, March 6, 2002.

11. Paul Charles Merkley, *Christian Attitudes towards the State of Israel* (Montreal: McGill–Queen's University Press, 2001), 200.

12. I do not mean to imply that Christian Zionism is a merely contemporary or simply American phenomenon. However, the movement's most profound effects have been contemporary and American. For recent detailed histories of the movement approached from slightly different perspectives, see Timothy P. Weber, *On the Road to Armageddon: How Evangelicals Became Israel's Best Friend* (Grand Rapids: Baker, 2004); and Stephen Sizer, *Christian Zionism: Road-Map to Armageddon?* (Leicester, U.K.: InterVarsity Press, 2004).

13. "The National Security Strategy of the United States," *New York Times*, September 20, 2002.

14. Irving Kristol, "The Neoconservative Persuasion," *Weekly Standard*, August 25, 2003. There was plenty of grist for the conspiracy mill: Vice President Richard Cheney and Undersecretary of Defense Douglas Feith have served on the board of the Jewish Institute for National Security Affairs (JINSA), while Cheney, Defense Secretary Donald Rumsfeld, and former Deputy Defense Secretary Paul Wolfowitz are affiliated with Project for a New American Century (PNAC), founded and chaired by *Weekly Standard* editor William Kristol. The neoconservative relationship with Israeli politics has been intimate.

15. James M. Inhofe, "Senate Floor Statement of Senator Inhofe: America's Stake in Israel's War on Terrorism," December 4, 2001.

16. Tom DeLay, "Be Not Afraid," July 30, 2003. In February of that year—the day the space shuttle *Columbia* disintegrated on reentry with Israeli astronaut Ilan Ramon aboard—DeLay expressed an even more profound self-identification with Israel, if not Judaism, by reciting, in Aramaic, the last lines of the *kaddish*, the Jewish prayer for the dead.

17. Kathleen Christison, *Perceptions of Palestine: Their Influence on US Middle East Policy* (Berkeley: University of California Press, 1999), 92–93.

18. Josef Federman, "Evangelical-Israeli Ties Make Rabbis Nervous," *Saint Paul (Minn.) Pioneer Press*, May 22, 2004. See also Yaakov Ariel, Philosemites or Antisemites? Evangelical Christian Attitudes toward Jews, Judaism, and the State of Israel, Analysis of Current Trends in Antisemitism 20 (Jerusalem: Vidal Sassoon International Center for the Study of Antisemitism, 2002). I am grateful to my colleague, Santiago Slabodsky, for this resource.

19. Robert O. Freedman is a political science professor at Baltimore Hebrew University. Quoted in Jeffery L. Sheler, "Odd Bedfellows," *U.S. News & World Report*, August 12, 2002, 34–35. See also the quote from Rabbi Eric Yoffie, president of the Union of American Hebrew Congregations: "To associate Israel with more extremist religious and political views may jeopardize the allegiance of mainstream Americans. That would be dangerous."

20. Cited in Merkley, *Christian Attitudes*, 204.

21. Ibid., 201.

22. Ibid., 215.

23. Ibid., 76–77, citing Naim S. Ateek, *Justice, and Only Justice: A Palestinian Theology of Liberation* (Maryknoll, N.Y.: Orbis, 1989), 77–78.

24. Ibid., 220.

25. Munib Younan, Bishop of the ELCJHL, has called Christian Zionism a heresy. See Ann E. Hafften, "Challenge the Implications of 'Christian Zionism,'" *Journal of Lutheran Ethics* 3(2) (February 2003).

26. Cited by Malcolm Foster, "Christian Zionists Feel the Heat for Fighting Peace: Extremists Wield Considerable Power within Republican Party," *Middle East & North Africa Daily Star*, July 26, 2003, 3.

27. Merkley, *Christian Attitudes*, 218; 217–18.

28. Cited in Wagner, "Reagan and Begin," 46. Information at www.jhm.org/exodus2.asp, accessed November 1, 2003.

29. Novik, *The United States and Israel*, 71.

30. Douglas Turner, "'Christian Zionists' Resist Bush on Mideast Peace," *Buffalo News*, August 17, 2003.

31. During his second term, President Bush agreed with Israeli Prime Minister Sharon's assessment that a unilateral departure from Gaza is a move toward peace and that the return of Palestinian refugees displaced in 1948 and 1967 is impractical. Those agreements took place in the shadow of Israel's "separation barrier"—decried by many Israeli and international human-rights organizations as another means for Israel to annex West Bank land desirable for Israeli purposes. These understandings were established in the exchange of letters between Bush and Sharon during the latter's visit to Washington, D.C., on April 14, 2004. One year later, during a meeting between the two leaders at Prairie Chapel Ranch near Crawford, Texas, Bush offered some mild criticism of Israeli policy. Referring to such Israeli government activities as barrier building and settlement expansion around Jerusalem, Bush reported, "I told the Prime Minister of my concern that Israel not undertake any activity that contravenes road map obligations or prejudice final status negotiations." See Office of the Press Secretary, "President and Prime Minister Sharon Discuss Economy, Middle East," April 11, 2005, www.whitehouse.gov.

32. Barbara R. Rossing, *The Rapture Exposed: The Message of Hope in the Book of Revelation* (Boulder, Colo.: Westview, 2004).

33. Clifton Kirkpatrick, "Statement from the Stated Clerk of the General Assembly of the Presbyterian Church (U.S.A.)," July 20, 2004, www.pcusa.org/oga/news.htm.

Chapter 4. The Call to Action

1. This survey, done by Israeli Media, was part of a study to explain what that organization regarded as a worldwide "media bias against Israel."

2. Pat McDonnell Twair, "Media Pro Greta Berlin Will Show Her PowerPoint Presentation Anywhere in U.S.," *Washington Report on Middle East Affairs*, October 2004, 63.

3. In a study of three American TV networks (ABC, CBS, NBC), American journalist Alison Weir found those networks' reporting of the conflict to be unbalanced. The study examined news of conflict-caused deaths of children in 2004 and found that deaths of Israeli children were reported at ratios about ten times those of Palestinian children's deaths. Two of the networks, ABC and NBC, reported on all eight of the Israeli children who died but on only 11 percent and 10 percent, respectively, of the 179 Palestinian children's deaths. A summary of the study appeared on the Web site of If Americans Knew, www.ifamericansknew.org.

4. The words war touches every discussion of the "security barrier" Israel is building in Palestinian territory. Its defenders prefer the word *fence*. Critics typically use *wall*, even *apartheid wall*. Says Ruvik Rosenthal, who writes a language column for the Israeli newspaper *Ma'ariv*, "The word *fence* unites Israelis who just want security. If you call it a wall, it just sounds ugly."

5. Official Israeli voices often describe Palestinians in language that meets no diplomatic-decency test. Lawrence Davidson, a history teacher at Pennsylvania's West Chester University, wrote in *CounterPunch*, April 3–5, 2004, "Descriptions of Palestinians by Israeli leaders range from 'there [is] no such thing as Palestinians' (Prime Minister Golda Meir, June 15, 1969) to 'people who do not belong to our continent, to our world, but actually belong to a different galaxy' (President Moshe Katsav, May 10, 2001). For a man like Prime Minister Ariel Sharon, 'peace' for Israel comes through dominating and controlling 'the enemies of humanity' (January 5, 2004)." This is not to say that many Palestinians don't reciprocate in similarly offensive language when speaking of Israeli Jews.

6. Available from Media Education Foundation, 60 Masonic St., Northamptom MA 01060. Or phone 800-897-0089, or send e-mail to info@mediaed.org. Cost: $30. For a list of videos, see Resources.

7. B'tselem, the Israeli Information Center for Human Rights in the Occupied Territories, reported that between September 29, 2000, and October 15, 2005, 974 Israelis (both civilians and military) had been killed by Palestinians; 3,334 Palestinians had died by action of Israeli military forces or civilians. For latest fatality statistics, see www.btselem.org.

8. Samuel W. Lewis, "The Receding Horizon: The Endless Quest for Arab-Israeli Peace," *Foreign Affairs*, September/October 2004. Dennis Ross is a U.S. diplomat who spent decades, under both Republican and Democrat administrations, pursuing Israeli-Arab peace. One perspective on the failure of Camp David under President Clinton is Ross's book *The Missing Peace: The Inside Story of the Fight for Middle East Peace* (New York: Farrar, Straus &

Giroux, 2004). For a quite different perspective, see Clayton E. Swisher, *The Truth about Camp David: The Untold Story about the Collapse of the Middle East Peace Process* (New York: Nation, 2004).

9. Joel Kovel, "In the Realm of the Double Standard," *Tikkun*, January-February 2003, 21. *Tikkun*, edited by Rabbi Michael Lerner, is "a bimonthly Jewish critique of politics, culture and society." Other observers have tied the U.S.–Iraq war itself to Israeli pressure. John K. Cooley, a former correspondent for the *Christian Science Monitor*, wrote in "The Israeli Factor," "For this writer, after covering [the Middle East] for nearly half a century, [this concern remains]. Our mainstream media, almost without exception, tip-toe around the role played by Israel in pushing the Bushites into war [with Iraq]" (*Link*, October-November 2005, 2). Other observers have linked the U.S.-Iraq war itself to Israeli interest. John K. Cooley, former correspondent for *The Christian Science Monitor* and ABC News, wrote in "The Israeli Factor," *The Link*, October-November 2005, 2: "...after covering Arab and Muslim regions for nearly half a century, [I have this concern]: Our mainstream media, almost without exception, tip-toe around the role played by Israel in pushing the Bushites into war [against Iraq] in March 2003."

10. Thomas H. Kean, Lee H. Hamilton, et al., *The 9/11 Report: The National Commission on Terrorist Attacks upon the United States* (New York: St. Martin's Paperbacks, 2004), 538.

11. Daniel Seidemann, *Washington Post* opinion article, "Letting Israel Self-Destruct," August 26, 2004.

12. Churches for Middle East Peace (CMEP) was launched in 1984 to share policy perspectives drawn from the Middle East experience of member bodies. Current members are the Alliance of Baptists, American Friends Service Committee, Antiochian Orthodox Archdiocese of North America, Armenian Orthodox Church, Catholic Conference of Major Superiors of Men's Institutes, Christian Church (Disciples of Christ), Church of the Brethren, Church World Service, Episcopal Church, Evangelical Lutheran Church in America, Franciscan Friars OFM, Friends Committee on National Legislation, Greek Orthodox Archdiocese of America, Maryknoll Missioners, Mennonite Central Committee, National Council of Churches of Christ, Presbyterian Church (U.S.A.), Reformed Church in America, Unitarian Universalist Association, United Church of Christ, United Methodist Church. CMEP's Web site is at www.cmep.org.

13. B'tselem, the Israeli Information Center for Human Rights, says that almost half a million Palestinians in the West Bank and East Jerusalem are directly burdened by the barrier's route—30,500 living on the west (Israeli) side of the barrier, 244,000 in "communities east of the barrier that are surrounded on at least three sides," and 216,000 in East Jerusalem totally separated from the West Bank. Statistics updated September 12, 2005, on B'tselem's Web site www.btselem.org.

14. Peter Steinfels, "Mideast Initiative Pushes beyond Platitudes," *New York Times*, December 6, 2003. Muslim leaders in the Initiative for Peace

include heads of the largest national Muslim organizations: Islamic Society of North America, Islamic Circle of North America, and the Council of Mosques. Jewish leaders include officials from the Conservative, Reform, and Reconstructionist rabbinical associations. Christians include two Roman Catholic cardinals, president of the U.S. Conference of Catholic Bishops, the primate of the Greek Orthodox Church, heads of Lutheran, United Methodist, Presbyterian, Episcopal, United Church of Christ, and Disciples denominations, plus prominent evangelical leaders.

15. Scott McConnell, "Kerry's the One," *American Conservative*, November 8, 2004.

16. Martha Sawyer Allen, "In the Crossfire," *Minneapolis Star Tribune*, June 21, 2003.

17. Bridges for Peace, "Dispatch from Jerusalem" (newsletter), November–December 2002, www.bridgesforpeace.com.

18. Marc H. Ellis, *O Jerusalem! The Contested Future of the Jewish Covenant* (Minneapolis: Fortress Press, 1999), 163.

19. *Living Stones Pilgrimage* is authored by two Christians who have lived and worked in the Holy Land: Allison Hilliard of the United Kingdom and Betty Bailey of the United States. It is available from Notre Dame Press (www. UNDPress.nd.edu). Bailey, a United Church of Christ minister, has a Web site "lead[ing] you to information and experiences that are alternative to mass tourism and mass media": www.holylandresources.net.

20. Daphna Berman, "Holy Land Crusaders of a Different Kind," *Ha'aretz*, October 15, 2004.

21. Good sources of information on ministries of Christian communities in Palestine: The Evangelical Lutheran Church of Jordan and the Holy Land (ELCJHL) is the Jerusalem-based, six-congregation body ministering in Jordan, Palestine, and Israel (www.holyland-lutherans.org). The International Center of Bethlehem is a program of Christmas Lutheran Church, one of the ELCJHL congregations (www.annadwa.org). The Lutheran World Federation operates health and educational ministries serving Palestinians (www.lwfjerusalem.org). The Middle East Council of Churches links four families of churches—Eastern Orthodox, Oriental Orthodox, Protestant, and Roman Catholic—for joint work in social ministries and interreligious relations (www.mec-churches.org). Based in Beirut, it has liaison offices in Cyprus, Egypt, Jordan, United Arab Emirates, and Jerusalem. Sabeel is the Palestinian Christian Center for Liberation Theology, a studies program supported by Palestinian and overseas Christians (www.sabeel.org).

22. Mitri Raheb, *Bethlehem Besieged: Stories of Hope in Times of Trouble* (Minneapolis: Fortress Press, 2004), 123.

23. "The Department of State continues to urge U.S. citizens to defer unnecessary travel to the West Bank and avoid all travel to Gaza," says the advisory that was current in late 2005. The Government of Israel may deny entry at Ben Gurion Airport or at a land border to persons it believes might travel to

'closed' areas . . . or to persons the Israeli authorities believe may sympathize with the Palestinian cause. . . . Major cities in the West Bank are often placed under Israeli military curfew." Current comment on security concerns can be found at www.usembassy-israel.org.il; click on "Latest Warden Message."

24. Raheb, *Bethlehem Besieged*, 118.

25. Ibid., 155.

26. Episcopal News Service, "Palestinian Christians Encourage Visits to Holy Land," August 30, 2004.

Appendix. Whose Land Is It?

Ronald D. Witherup, S.S., a Sulpician priest and provincial of the U.S. Province of the Society of Saint Sulpice, is president of the Conference of Major Superiors of Men (CMSM). The umbrella group of leadership of U.S. Catholic men's orders, CMSM is a member of Churches for Middle East Peace. His essay is adapted from a slightly longer article that appeared in CMSM Forum 87 (spring 2003) and is reprinted with the author's permission.

1. A recent comprehensive study is Michael Prior, *The Bible and Colonialism: A Moral Critique*, The Biblical Seminar 48 (Sheffield, U.K.: Sheffield Academic Press, 1997). Other major works include W. D. Davies, *The Gospel and the Land: Early Christian and Jewish Territorial Doctrine* (Berkeley: University of California Press, 1974) and *The Territorial Dimensions of Judaism* (Berkeley: University of California Press, 1982); and Walter Brueggemann, *The Land* (Philadelphia: Fortress Press, 1977). A complete bibliography appears in the Prior volume. For a convenient short article on the land, see W. Janzen, "Land," *Anchor Bible Dictionary* (New York: Doubleday, 1992), 4:143–54.

2. The term *holy land* occurs only once in the Old Testament (Zechariah 2:12), where it refers to an eschatological kingdom.

3. The New Testament's perspective is not considered here. Suffice it to say that the concrete notion of the land eventually becomes spiritualized, evolving into an eschatological perspective of the new kingdom of Jesus Christ and a "heavenly Jerusalem" (Hebrews 12:22; Revelation 3:12; 21:2; 21:10).

4. Note that the Hebrew does not have a word for "promise." The expression "promised land," which does not occur in the Bible, is really an interpretive extension of the Old Testament notion that God spoke about the land as part of the covenant with the Israelites.

Index of Scripture

New Testament

Index of Subjects and Names